SUMMARY

Yemen is not currently a failed state, but it is experiencing huge political and economic problems that can have a direct impact on U.S. interests in the region. It has a rapidly expanding population with a resource base that is limited and already leaves much of the current population in poverty. The government obtains around a third of its budget revenue from sales of its limited and declining oil stocks, which most economists state will be exhausted by 2017. Yemen has critical water shortages aggravated by the use of extensive amounts of water and agricultural land for production of the shrub *qat*, which is chewed for stimulant and other effects but has no nutritional value. All of these problems are especially difficult to address because the central government has only limited capacity to extend its influence into tribal areas beyond the capital and major cities. Adding to these difficulties, Yemen is also facing a variety of interrelated national security problems that have strained the limited resources of the government, military, and security forces. In Sa'ada province in Yemen's northern mountainous region, there has been an intermittent rebellion by Houthi tribesmen who accuse the government of discrimination and other actions against their Zaydi Shi'ite religious sect. In southern Yemen, a powerful independence movement has developed which is mostly nonviolent but is also deeply angry and increasingly confrontational.

A key country that must be considered in formulating Yemen policy is Saudi Arabia. Riyadh is Yemen's chief aid donor and often considers itself to have a special relationship with Yemen that affords it an elevated and privileged role in providing external guidance to Sana'a. Some observers suggest that Saudi Arabia views this role as so important that challenging Saudi interests in Yemen is sometimes viewed as equally offensive as interfering in Saudi domestic politics. Riyadh has become especially sensitive about Yemen issues in recent years and even intervened militarily on the side of the Yemeni government in the most recent phase of the Houthi war in Sa'ada province. The Saudis are also deeply involved with Yemen in the struggle against al-Qaeda due in part to a 2009 merger of the Saudi and Yemeni branches of this organization. The merger occurred following the decision of Saudi al-Qaeda members to flee to Yemen to rebuild their battered organization. Saudi Arabia's special relationship with Yemen can both help and hinder U.S. objectives for that country.

Additionally, Yemen's government has waged a struggle against al-Qaeda with vacillating levels of intensity since at least 2001 when its leadership chose to cooperate with the United States on counterterrorism concerns in the aftermath of the September 11, 2001, strikes. More recently, Yemen has emerged as one of the most important theaters for the struggle against al-Qaeda, as many members of this organization attempt to regroup and reorganize themselves in Yemen after suffering crippling setbacks in Saudi Arabia, Pakistan, and Afghanistan. The loss of Yemen to al-Qaeda would be particularly damaging to Western interests due to its strategic location and a population which is expected to exceed half of that of the entire Arabian Peninsula within the next 20 years. Moreover, al-Qaeda in the Arabian Peninsula (AQAP), headquartered in Yemen, appears to be strengthening and showing signs of transitioning from a terrorist group with limited capabilities to an emerging insurgent movement.

Yemen is also an especially distrustful and wary nation in its relationship with Western nations, and particularly the United States. Most Yemenis are fiercely protective of their country's independence from outside influence, especially from countries that they believe do not always have the best interests of the Arab World in mind. While Yemen's government is coming to understand the dangers it faces from al-Qaeda, the struggle against this organization is not always popular among the Yemeni public, and any large-scale U.S. military presence in the country could easily ignite these passions and destabilize the regime. Under such circumstances, it is important to help Yemen, but to do so in ways that are not viewed as intrusive or dominating by a population that does not always identify with U.S. concerns about international terrorism. In recent years, U.S. policymakers have managed to maintain this balance, but the complexities of Yemeni domestic politics will continue to require subtlety and nimbleness in U.S.-Yemeni security relations.

THE CONFLICTS IN YEMEN AND U.S. NATIONAL SECURITY

As President, I have made it a priority to strengthen our partnership with the Yemeni government — training and equipping their security forces, sharing intelligence, and working with them to strike al-Qaeda terrorists.

> President Barack Obama,
> January 2010[1]

Yemen stands out from its neighbors on the Arabian Peninsula. The inability of the Yemeni government to secure and exercise control over all of its territory offers terrorist and insurgent groups in the region, particularly al-Qaeda, a safe haven from which to plan, organize, and support terrorist operations.

> General David Petraeus,
> April 2009[2]

As soon as the [United States] comes down into our land and comes to colonize us, jihad is obligatory according to our religion.

> Sheikh Abdul Majeed Zindani,
> leading Yemeni cleric, January 2010[3]

INTRODUCTION

The United States is currently deeply concerned with the need to contain and defeat al-Qaeda forces in Yemen. Nevertheless, it seems impossible to formulate a meaningful strategy to meet this objective without carefully considering a variety of other important factors which have come to dominate Yemeni politics. These factors include a crippled and declining econo-

1

my, as well as recurring problems with national unity. Currently, Yemen faces simmering unrest in the north that sometimes leads to revolt among Houthi tribesmen and a strong but mostly nonviolent secessionist movement in the south. Under these conditions, U.S. policy must be informed by a deep understanding of both Yemen's domestic politics and current Yemeni government capacity to enforce its laws and maintain internal security. U.S. policy formulations must also be based on a solid understanding of the constraints that influence Yemen's leadership, especially the nuances of Yemen's relations with its most influential neighbor, Saudi Arabia, and the views of the Yemeni public on both al-Qaeda and U.S. objectives in the region.

The tasks associated with developing and implementing effective policy for Yemen are challenging. Yemen is remote from the United States and has traditionally generated little interest in Washington. Until recently, it has seldom been linked to important U.S. national interests. Moreover, Yemeni values and attitudes have been formed within a very different type of society than those of the West. The potential for distrust, misunderstanding, and miscommunication is therefore strong, although the importance of the U.S-Yemeni relationship has seldom been greater, due to a variety of factors including the rise of al-Qaeda in that country. Fortunately, while Yemeni society and politics are complex, they are also comprehensible. Moreover, well-informed U.S. planning efforts to help Yemen and ensure stability in the Arabian Peninsula are clearly possible.

This work hopes to provide an overview of many of the most important issues that must be considered when addressing Yemen policy, as well as suggesting possible approaches to obtaining important U.S. and Yemeni goals in the region. It is hoped that the reader will find this work useful in understanding and untangling many of the complexities of the Yemeni political, economic, and international situations that touch upon key U.S. and Western interests.

THE YEMENI POLITICAL SYSTEM IN CRISIS

Yemen is a large and strategically important country in the southern Arabian Peninsula bordering Saudi Arabia, Oman, the Red Sea, and the Gulf of Aden within the Arabian Sea. It is also the poorest country in the Arab World, with a population that has been unrelentingly resistant to significant central government involvement in local affairs (except to provide resources). The territory outside of the capital of Sana'a is difficult for a national authority to control due to restive, well-armed, and powerful tribes spread across a diverse geography, including vast desert areas and extremely rugged mountains. These tribes have at various points in their history resisted the authority of the Ottoman Turks, British military forces in the south, and various Yemeni governments that they judged as being too heavy-handed in their relations with tribal leaders. Historically, Yemeni tribes have also been willing to show conditional loyalty to national government authorities that avoid taxing them and that provide them with gifts of money, weapons, and other forms of support. A frequent and sly comment on the political culture is that loyalty is rented in Yemen rather than bought.

Yemen is currently the only nonmonarchy on the Arabian Peninsula, as well as one of that region's most heavily populated countries.[4] Its population of

23,500,000 is almost comparable with that of Saudi Arabia, and the birth rates of both countries suggest that Yemen is rapidly becoming the most populous country in the Gulf. The Yemeni population is currently growing by around 3.45 percent per year, and is expected to reach 38 million in the next 15 years.[5] Yemen's poverty, political geography, republican form of government, and large and rapidly expanding population distinguish it from the other states of the Arabian Peninsula, including the wealthy, sparsely-populated monarchies. Yemeni society is composed of two major Islamic sects which are variants on the traditional Sunni and Shi'ite forms of Islam found elsewhere. Yemen's current president, Ali Abdullah Saleh, is a member of Yemen's Shi'ite Muslim sect, known as Zaydis. The monarchy that his republican predecessors overthrew in 1962 was also governed by a Zaydi imam and his circle. Around a third of Yemen's population is composed of Zaydis, the dominant group in the northern part of the country. Yemen's form of Sunni Islam is known as Shafeism. Shafeism and Zaydism share many similarities in doctrine and rituals, and the gap between the sects has narrowed in the last few decades due to state efforts to stress cooperation between sects. Zaydi beliefs and rituals are usually considered to have much less in common with the Twelver Shi'ism practiced in Iran and Iraq than with Yemeni Shafeism.

Yemen's years as a republic began with a September 1962 military *coup d'état* in what was then the separate country of North Yemen (the Yemen Arab Republic [YAR]).[6] This coup's leadership overthrew a traditional imamate that had ruled the area either independently or under formal Ottoman sovereignty for over 1,000 years.[7] The new leadership consisted of leftist military officers who were heavily influenced by the Arab nationalist and anti-imperialist rhetoric of Egyptian president, Gamal Abdul Nasser. [8] Correspondingly, the 1962 change in government (often called a revolution) was strongly supported by the Egyptian government, which viewed the imam's ouster in ideological terms, whereby a pro-Egyptian modernizing military elite would replace a reactionary monarchical leader.[9] The imam's ouster also led to a long and bloody civil war between the new government (supported by a large Egyptian expeditionary force) and tribal rebels seeking the restoration of the imamate.[10] At the height of their involvement in Yemen, Egyptian forces included at least 60,000 troops which made use of chemical warfare to combat tribal-based opposition to the new government.[11] Conversely, royalist fighters received substantial military and financial aid from Saudi Arabia and made exceptionally good use of the difficult terrain of the northern Yemeni mountains. This conflict lasted almost 8 years and concluded only in 1970, although Egyptian forces had withdrawn several years earlier, following Cairo's massive June 1967 defeat by Israel.[12] The North Yemen Civil War was widely described as "Nasser's Vietnam."[13]

Somewhat surprisingly, North Yemen's republican government survived in office following the withdrawal of Egyptian troops from that country. The government's ability to retain formal authority and at least some power was partially made possible by divisions and infighting among the tribes that had opposed it. North Yemen's republic also survived due to strong governmental efforts to establish acceptable relations with enough of these tribes to avoid a final confrontation against them. The Yemeni government further moved decisively to improve its relations with

Riyadh and thereby halt outside funding for the rebellion. Republican compromise with the tribes and Saudi Arabia thus prevented the development of a powerful Yemeni government and assured that the Sana'a leadership curbed their ideas about extending their authority and modernizing the country.[14] Elsewhere in the Arabian Peninsula, South Yemen became independent in 1967 after 128 years as an amalgam of protectorates of the United Kingdom.[15] This newly independent country then established itself as the Peoples Democratic Republic of Yemen (PDRY), the Arab World's first Marxist government, and quickly moved to establish close relations with the Soviet bloc. Later, South Yemen gave up its separate existence and merged with the more populous North Yemen in 1990. This was done primarily from a well-founded fear of economic bankruptcy and political isolation following the loss of aid due to the then impending collapse of the Soviet Union. Political and ideological differences between northern and southern Yemenis were expected to be addressed and resolved through a system of political democracy including multiparty elections. With this future environment in mind, a number of southern Yemeni leaders entered the union in the expectation that they would play an important role in the new government and that the Yemeni electorate would quickly come to view them as the true modernizers. Such expectations were dashed when they were increasingly overshadowed and then marginalized by former North Yemeni President Ali Abdullah Saleh, who had retained his position as president and the head of state in the newly united Yemen. Saleh's political party, the General People's Congress (GPC), dramatically outperformed the Yemeni Socialist Party (YSP) in the April 1993 Parliamentary elections, help-

ing him to consolidate power and marginalize southern rivals.[16] For reasons to be examined later, this was
to be the last election where the YSP was an important
competitor.[17]

Despite the views of many southern Yemenis
about the self-evident superiority of socialism, President Saleh's political skills at marginalizing his southern competitors should not have come as a surprise
to anyone. Saleh had taken power in North Yemen
in July 1978, more than a decade prior to the merger,
replacing caretaker president Abdul Karim al-Arashi,
who served for only 3 weeks before turning his position over to Saleh. Although Arashi served for an
exceptionally brief period, he at least walked away
with his life. The two Yemeni presidents serving in
the years immediately prior to Arashi's pathetic term
were both assassinated as a result of the turbulent
Arabian Peninsula politics of that era. Arashi's imme-
diate predecessor, President Ahmad al-Ghashmi (in
office 1977-78) was murdered by an envoy from South
Yemen in what appears to have been part of a power
struggle in the PDRY. The preceding president, Ibra-
him al-Hamdi (in office 1974-77), was assassinated by
an individual who is widely believed to have been a
Saudi agent. The Riyadh leaders at that time feared
that the North Yemeni president was seeking a rapprochement with the PDRY that could have become a
serious national security threat to them.[18] Saleh himself became president at age 35 and was not widely expected to survive for long in the top job. Nevertheless,
he defied these low expectations and has remained in
power ever since that time through brilliant political
skills and personal toughness. Later, as previously
noted, Saleh became president of a united Yemen in
1990 when North and South Yemen merged. He has

remained in that position ever since, outmaneuvering all domestic opponents and using the military to crush a 1994 attempt by southern leaders to secede from a united Yemen in a 10-week civil war.

Saleh's longevity in power and craftiness as president has nevertheless not made governing Yemen easier over time, or allowed him to consolidate power as the leader of a powerful and well-organized autocratic regime. It is consequently impossible to consider him to be a strong president such as Egyptian leader Hosni Mubarak, let alone a despot like former Iraqi dictator, Saddam Hussein. Rather, President Saleh compares his efforts to balance the often competing concerns of Yemen's tribes, religious groups, political factions, and interested outside powers to "dancing on the heads of snakes," a continuous struggle to make exactly the right moves to avoid serious confrontations with powerful political groups, families, and tribes.[19]

Others sometimes suggest his tactics are more like a divide and rule strategy, expertly exploiting and sometimes widening the fissures in Yemeni society. In this struggle, the president's chief tool of governance is a network of patronage relationships and subsidies provided to friendly individuals, families, and tribes in exchange for support.[20] The government sometimes uses police and military repression to enforce its policies, but this approach is usually a last resort which cannot always be applied efficiently and effectively within strongly tribalized regions. Yemen consequently runs on a system of tribal subsidies and bribes, with tribal leaders consistently showing an interest in money that supersedes concerns about religion, ideology, or politics.[21] In essence, tribal leaders base their support for the government on how much it is willing to provide to them.

Additionally, throughout Saleh's time in office, Yemen has often been described as a "family regime," in which the president's relatives and members of his Sahhan tribe have steadily been placed in a number of key national security positions in order to protect the regime. This approach is a partial hedge against the system of rented loyalty and shifting alliances that characterize Yemeni political culture. Unsurprisingly, in this environment, the president's oldest son, Colonel Ahmed Ali Saleh, is expected to become a serious contender for the office of president upon his father's death or retirement. Currently, Colonel Saleh is the commander of Yemen's Republican Guard and the Yemeni Army's elite Special Forces units. In addition to placing his son in this key position, President Saleh appointed his half-brother as the commander of the Yemeni Air Force, while the president's nephews command the Central Security Organization (CSO) and the Presidential Guards.[22] Another leading regime figure is Brigadier General Ali Mushin al-Ahmar, who is sometimes identified as the second most powerful individual within the government. He is often described as a "kinsman" of President Saleh, although the exact nature of their family ties is unclear.[23] Mushin has played a significant role in many key regime policies, including the recruitment of Yemenis to fight in the anti-Soviet war in Afghanistan.[24] He has also played a major role in leading the military struggle against Houthi rebels in the northern part of the country.[25]

Within the labyrinth of regime and family politics, succession is an increasingly important issue. President Saleh is currently in his late 60s (born on March 21, 1942), and was most recently reelected to his post in a September 2006 election for an additional 7-year term in office.[26] It is not known if he will seek another term in office in 2013 at the age of 71. To do so may require an amendment to the Yemeni Constitution or perhaps a friendly legal interpretation of the eligibility requirements regarding a sitting president's ability to seek a third term in office.[27] Some solution of this sort should be obtainable if Saleh decides to seek reelection. Nevertheless, at some point, the current president will not be able to continue to serve in office. At that juncture, whoever ultimately follows Saleh will face Yemen's exceptionally serious economic and security problems, with fewer carefully nurtured domestic alliances and less political experience than Saleh currently possesses. The new leadership will also have to consolidate power within the system of political, tribal, and personal relationships that Saleh has constructed throughout his years in power. The president's son, Ahmed Saleh, is something of an unknown as a political leader, and his skills at managing and manipulating Yemeni power centers are untested. Perhaps shrewdly, the younger Saleh has maintained a low public profile in Yemeni politics despite the possibility that he may have a solid claim to be the presidential heir apparent. Ahmed probably made this choice in the knowledge that bloodless coups by sons against their aging fathers are not unknown in the contemporary Arab World.[28] While there is no evidence that President Saleh is concerned about Ahmed's activities, it may be useful for any careful son to seek no more than reflected glory under such sensitive conditions.

In addition to being a highly tribalized nation, Yemen has the most well-armed society in the Middle East. Virtually all Yemeni men have rifles, and one's standing within rural Yemeni tribal communities is often enhanced by the possession of high quality fire-

arms and other personal weapons such as hand gre-
nades. Yemeni tribes have often been able to obtain
crew-served weapons, including machine guns and
mortars. Reacting to this excess, Yemen's government
has attempted to institute some curbs on weapons
possession and publicly carrying small arms over
the past few years. These efforts have been of limited scope and effectiveness. Openly carrying assault
rifles and similar weapons in cities was prohibited
in 2007, and some firearms markets (apparently operating without government permission) were also
closed in that year.[29] These measures had no practical
impact on the availability of weapons throughout the
country. Moreover, the most heavily armed segment
of Yemen's population lives in rural areas, and these
people often view possession of small arms as essen-
tial for their security. Correspondingly, any extensive
efforts to regulate weapons more aggressively could
meet a serious backlash and would remain unenforce-
able in the areas of the country that the government
does not control.

Even more alarming than the issue of unregulated
small arms is the state of the Yemeni economy. Yemen's economic system is currently under severe
strain and may be in danger of collapsing if ongoing
trends are not reversed. In addition to worldwide
problems created by the global economic recession,
Yemen is faced with diminishing oil resources, an ex-
ploding population, an escalating strain on water resources, and other serious economic problems. Sana'a,
in particular, is widely expected to be hit by especially
severe water shortages in the next decade.[30] Unemployment is also at a shocking 35 percent, according to
a 2010 interview with Yemeni Prime Minister Ali Mohammed Megwar.[31] Sadly, under these circumstances,

the Yemeni middle class has been steadily shrinking over the last decade, and this destabilizing trend is expected to continue without significant new sources of income. Hunger and malnutrition are already serious problems, with the potential to become significantly worse. According to the United Nations (UN) World Food Program, around 7.2 million Yemenis suffer from chronic hunger, and the possibility of famine exists.[32]

Additionally, Yemen would clearly face an even more severe employment crisis without its bloated public sector employment, although many of these jobs are unproductive and contribute little or nothing to economic development.[33] Adding to these problems, Yemen already has an extremely young population, with almost 44 percent of its population under age 14, and current population growth trends will dramatically increase the Yemeni youth bulge with no clear corresponding ability to provide jobs for these young people.[34] Large groups of unemployed youth may also become a major force for instability.

Yemen reached peak oil production in 2004, and its output has been decreasing since that time. Currently, the Yemeni economy produces less than 300,000 barrels of oil per day of which around half is exported.[35] The revenues obtained through these exports usually contribute around three-quarters of the funding for the national budget.[36] Unfortunately, Yemen has responded to falling oil revenues by increasing the exploitation of its two major oil fields of Masilah and Safar in an attempt to compensate for their declining output and maintain a steady source of government funds.[37] This approach has some short-term financial advantages, but more ominously suggests the possibility of an almost total production crash around 2017.[38]

Other sources of hard currency are equally problematic. The Yemenis have only recently begun efforts to export liquefied natural gas, and it remains uncertain how successful this effort will be.[39] The once-promising tourism sector has been partially undermined by occasional incidents where terrorists have killed or kidnapped tourists for a variety of reasons, including disapproval of the policies of the tourists' home country.[40] The past tribal practice of kidnapping foreigners and treating them well while using them as a bargaining chip to gain concessions from the government still occurs, but there are now more brutal kidnappings that sometime result in the prisoners' deaths, as well as the direct tourist assassinations where there is no intent to kidnap, only to kill.[41]

The expanding Yemeni population and possible collapse in export income have implications for resource distribution, including that of water and food, but such systemic issues are not the only dimensions of these problems. Looming water shortages are also a result of misplaced agricultural priorities, including the excessive cultivation of the shrub, *qat* (*catha edulis*), which requires large amounts of water and good agricultural land but has no nutritional value. *Qat* has been cultivated in Yemen for at least 600 years as a chewed stimulant, which produces a feeling of euphoria after several hours followed by a state of mental depression.[42] It is often described by both Yemenis and non-Yemenis as a mild narcotic, although this classification seems to be one of convenience rather than medical fact. According to the Yemeni Deputy Prime Minister for Economic Affairs, "Though it is not a drug as many believe, it has many harmful effects, especially when it takes up a major proportion of the family's spending at the expense of food and schooling."[43] While the tragedy of wasting water and land resources on qat is apparent to many government planners, no Yemeni government has ever been able to impose serious constraints on its cultivation and use, which is deeply entrenched in Yemeni society. Around three-quarters of all Yemeni men use qat regularly and usually spend a significant percentage of their income to do so. While it has not always been socially acceptable for women to chew *qat*, this outlook is changing and the number of women users is now expanding.[44] Unsurprisingly, qat is one of the most lucrative cash crops for Yemeni farmers.

An additional Yemeni problem with both political and economic dimensions is corruption, which is so pervasive that some analysts have labeled the Yemeni political system a "kleptocracy," in which most officials use their positions to enrich themselves, their families, and key associates.[45] The system of corruption begins with hundreds of thousands of lower-ranking and badly paid government employees and soldiers who seek small bribes in the performance of their duties, to the much more important tribal leaders, government officials, businessmen, and military officers who are able to conduct corrupt activities on a much larger scale.[46] The low pay of ordinary soldiers and junior government officials tends to bias the system toward corrupt practices, which many people find necessary simply to survive. More senior officials naturally have greater opportunities for corruption, which they often exploit to the maximum extent possible. These circumstances are reflected on most recent Corruption Perceptions Index of the international watchdog organization Transparency International, which gives Yemen an abysmal ranking of 154 out of 180 countries (with 1 being the best rating for controlling corruption).[47] Moreover, Yemeni ratings have been getting progressively worse over the last few years, and are a potential indicator of cripplingly dysfunctional levels of corruption throughout the political and economic systems. It should be noted, however, that some, and perhaps many, Yemeni public officials chose to limit their corrupt activities and others may not be corrupt at all.[48] Even this degree of restraint may disappear if the Yemeni economy continues to decline as is widely expected.

As Yemen's middle class continues to shrink and nationwide poverty deepens, it is unclear how tolerant Yemeni society will remain of continuing corrupt practices, the most significant of which benefit only a limited number of political elites. The public may have already become cynical about reform due to the half-hearted, duplicitous, and ineffective measures to control corruption in the past. In the late 1990s, for example, the government announced efforts to move forward on issues such as reducing bribery, improving the efficiency of government bureaucrats, and eliminating unnecessary jobs. Unfortunately, the campaign soon emerged as a disguised purge that allowed the president to oust senior officials whose loyalty to him may have been in doubt, while increasing the security of his senior aides and closest associates.[49]

YEMEN'S SECURITY CONCERNS WITH THE HOUTHI REBELLION AND THE SOUTHERN SECESSIONISTS

Yemeni leaders, including the president, publicly maintain that fighting al-Qaeda forces in Yemen is their country's "first priority" for national security.[50] Such assurances are almost certainly misstatements designed to placate the United States, Saudi Arabia, and other interested countries and particularly to re-assure those countries that provide aid to Yemen.[51] Behind such declarations, the Sana'a government, and especially the population, have conventionally seen the actions of al-Qaeda as primarily a set of Western and Saudi problems.[52] This perception has now faded significantly among many senior government officials in recent years due to an escalation of the fighting between al-Qaeda and the security forces. Unfortunately, much of the population remains unconvinced that al-Qaeda is a serious threat since the organization does not usually target nongovernmental Yemeni civilians. Of course, civilians have suffered collateral deaths in al-Qaeda operations against security targets, and civilian deaths are sometimes collateral to infrastructure attacks.[53] Many Yemeni civilians also believe that the growth of al-Qaeda's strength throughout the region is a natural response to legitimate Arab anger over U.S. policies in the Middle East, particularly regarding Israel, the Palestinians, and Iraq. In a further complication, Yemeni news media commentators have frequently expressed their belief that the United States is insufficiently concerned about civilian collateral damage in its struggle against al-Qaeda throughout the Islamic World.[54]

The Yemeni government also faces other security concerns which its leaders may view as more threatening than al-Qaeda. These two concerns are an intermittent rebellion by northern Zaydi tribesmen, known as Houthis, and the separate and growing secessionist movement in the southern part of the country in what was formerly the PDRY. The Houthi rebellion is currently experiencing a shaky cease-fire, which the government publicly refers to as a permanent end to the conflict. This interpretation seems doubtful for reasons which will be discussed below. Either of these conflicts has the potential to sap the already steeply diminished energies of the Yemeni government and security forces, thereby rendering them less effective in fighting terrorism and supporting policies of internal economic development. The continuation of both conflicts would be especially difficult for Sana'a.

The Houthi Rebellion.

The Houthi rebellion has its origins with nonviolent anti-government demonstrations that broke out in Sa'ada province in northern Yemen in January 2003 under the leadership of Hussein al-Houthi, a prominent northern political leader, who was also one of the first members of the Yemeni parliament. At that time, the Houthi establishment and its supporters had become increasingly alienated from the Yemeni government over what they characterized as economic discrimination against their home province of Sa'ada in the north, as well as the government's excessive tolerance of Saudi-inspired anti-Shi'ite agitation in northern Yemen. These activities included the white-hot rhetoric of Saudi-trained anti-Shi'ite clerics who were sponsored and heavily funded by the Riyadh government.[55] Many assertive Salafi clerics maintain that the Zaydis and all other Shi'ites are heretics and apostates from true Islam.

In the aftermath of the January 2003 demonstrations, President Saleh unsuccessfully attempted to negotiate some sort of reconciliation with Hussein al-Houthi. Meanwhile anti-government demonstrations continued and even spread to the Grand Mosque in Sana'a. The conflict also intensified in the north with increasingly angry demonstrations there. While the Houthis had serious grievances related to their region, they challenged Saleh on a more direct and fundamental level by accusing the Yemeni government of placing itself in the service of the United States and Israel at the expense of Arab and Yemeni interests. Saleh viewed such charges as close to treasonous and was especially concerned because they came at a time of widespread Yemeni anger over the U.S.-led 2003 invasion of Iraq and the continuing unpopularity of Yemeni cooperation with the United States in the "war on terror." The rebels also continued to maintain that their region had been victimized by ongoing governmental discrimination and received limited public resources when compared to other parts of Yemen. Under these circumstances, Saleh lost his patience with negotiations and unsuccessfully moved to have Houthi arrested. This failed move led to the outbreak of war.

The first round of sustained fighting in Sa'ada took place from June 18 until September 10, 2004. After the move against Houthi, he and his political organization, the "Believing Youth" (*Shabab al-Moumineen*) moved to expel government troops and bureaucrats from Sa'ada. The government responded to Houthi acts of rebellion by increasing its military presence in the northern area, with fighting continuing in the north until Hussein al-Houthi's death in September 2004. The conflict has repeatedly reignited and continued sporadically since that time, with the rebels led by al-Houthi's brothers, including Abdul Malik al-Houthi. Qatar helped to negotiate a cease-fire in 2007 and a more comprehensive peace deal in 2008, but these agreements eventually broke down, and a new government military campaign was initiated in Sa'ada province on August 11, 2009, under the menacing name, Operation Scorched Earth.

The conflict with the Houthis then assumed a new dimension, with direct Saudi Arabian military intervention in the northern Yemeni fighting in November 2009 when some of the rebels crossed into Saudi territory, killing at least two border guards and apparently taking control of two or more Saudi border villages.[56] These audacious actions provoked a strong Saudi response based on the Riyadh leadership's anger over the aggressive violation of its sovereignty and the special concerns they harbor about hostile forces based in Yemen.

Yemen has a 700-mile border with Saudi Arabia, porous in many places, that can be used by criminals, smugglers, terrorists, and insurgents. The easy availability of arms in Yemen is a further complication, with most of the illegal weapons and explosives smuggled into Saudi Arabia coming from Yemen. The Saudis watched the Sa'ada conflict anxiously, becoming especially concerned when Houthi forces crossed into Saudi territory. Houthi spokesmen stated that they had crossed into Saudi Arabia because Riyadh had allowed the Yemeni military to use Saudi territory to wage war against them.[57] In response, Riyadh took decisive action, with Saudi military strikes against Houthi rebels rapidly unfolding as the largest combat operation that they had undertaken since the 1991 Gulf War. Saudi tactics in this conflict involved the heavy use of artillery and airpower bombardment followed by the deployment of infantry in mopping up operations.[58] The strategy behind this form of warfare was to employ firepower to destroy large elements of the Houthi forces so that Saudi infantry could more easily defeat the residual military forces.

Such tactics were only partially successful. The Saudi army reported that at least 133 of its soldiers were killed in action, with an undisclosed number of others wounded or captured in the fighting.[59] The Saudis discontinued their military involvement in the war in February 2010 when the Houthis withdrew from Saudi territory, a cease-fire involving both the Yemeni and Saudi governments was established, and all Saudi prisoners were returned.[60]

The Houthis agreed to the six point truce with the Sana'a leadership in February 2010, although it is unclear how long such a truce can be maintained. The Yemeni government did not address major Houthi grievances over discrimination and lack of development aid, and it is uncertain whether it will seek to do so at a later time. Despite these unresolved problems, President Saleh has attempted to project optimism on this issue, maintaining that "we can say the war is over; not stopped or in a truce." [61] Nevertheless, few informed observers view this result as likely without an intensive and ongoing governmental campaign to consolidate peaceful relations. Such concerns seem to have been underscored in July 2010 when 4 days of serious fighting again broke out between Houthis and either regular army troops or auxiliary government tribesmen who had been fighting beside the Yemeni army.[62] At least 40 people were killed in this fighting, according to sources on both sides.[63] The conflict was then finally brought under control by tribal mediators.

Despite the problems noted above, there have also been serious efforts to maintain the truce. The Qatari government, in particular, chose to recommit itself to the struggle for peace in northern Yemen, falling back upon its familiar role as mediator. In late August 2010, the Qataris sponsored a meeting in Doha in which the two sides agreed to an "explanatory appendix" associated with the earlier agreement.[64] The signing of this document by representatives of both the Yemeni government and the Houthi leadership was dutifully witnessed by Qatar's Prime Minister and Foreign Minister. The main goal of the Houthis in these negotiations was to obtain the release of around 1,000 prisoners who had been taken in the fighting in the north. The government agreed to meet this Houthi demand, and in return the Houthis agreed to surrender captured government weapons to Qatari mediators.[65]

The Yemeni government disputes Houthi claims that their recurring rebellions have been a response to continuous discrimination against the northern region and that they never sought to overthrow the Yemeni republic. Rather, Sana'a charges that the Houthis initiated the conflict in order to return Yemen to the days when it was ruled by a Zaydi imam, and that they would select such an imam from the senior leadership of the Houthi family. Additionally, while President Saleh is a Zaydi and therefore a member of the same Islamic sect as the Houthis, his lineage is not distinguished, and someone with his family background would not be eligible to become a Yemeni imam even if a non-Houthi was chosen.[66]

Saleh would never wish to achieve such status, however, since he is particularly contemptuous of the traditional stratified structure of Zaydi society associated with the imamate. Conversely, throughout the conflict, rebellious Houthis have often maintained that President Saleh has betrayed his co-religionists and it is therefore their right to defend themselves against the excesses of his regime. The right to rebel against an unjust leader is deeply ingrained in Zaydi doctrine, history, and tradition.[67] Moreover, the Houthis gained some moral high ground in the conflict since their attacks have been directed at Yemeni military and governmental targets, although this approach is not surprising as the fighting occurred on Houthi home terrain.

Houthi leaders have made considerable use of anti-U.S. and anti-Israeli rhetoric during previous rounds of fighting and have particularly enjoyed excoriating President Saleh for his ties with Washington, which they refer to as an alliance. While these criticisms may embarrass the Saleh regime with the Yemeni public, they also make it significantly easier for his government to characterize the Houthis as radicals and terrorists before an international audience. Such charges come in an interesting context. There is no evidence linking the Houthis to al-Qaeda, and they are known to be bitterly hostile to that organization and all Salafi jihadists. The Yemeni government has therefore not wasted its effort or credibility by attempting to link the Houthis with al-Qaeda terrorists.

They have, however, frequently accused Iran of backing the Houthi rebels with funding, training, and material aid. Yemen further claims that such support is provided either directly by Iran or through Arabic speaking surrogates such as the radical Lebanese group Hezbollah. [68] The Iranian leadership reinforces this perception with rhetorical support for the Houthis in a policy of religious solidarity. It is difficult to imagine that they could remain silent on an issue so important to the Shi'ite community.[69] Yemen's charges involving Iranian materiel support and training have not been proven and may be at least partially based on the fact that the rebels are Shi'ite, although they are Fiver Shi'ites rather than the Twelver Shi'ites found in Iran. Yemeni government officials have sometime charged that the Houthi leadership seeks to move its followers away from the principles and practices of moderate Shi'ite Islam to a more militant form of

Twelver Shi'ism modeled after the Iranian approach to religion.[70] The Yemeni government has also accused Libya of supporting the Houthi rebels, but provided no credible evidence to support these accusations.[71]

The nature of the Sa'ada conflict may have created difficulties for the prospect of permanent Houthi reconciliation with the government. The Yemeni army does not have a well-developed doctrine for counterinsurgency, and Houthi civilian casualties have often been reported to be heavy. The Houthis claim to have suffered over 25,000 deaths at the hands of the Yemeni military since 2003, although other estimates are significantly lower.[72] Critics of the Saleh government have gone so far as to state that civilians are deliberately targeted by government forces and pro-government auxiliary units.[73] Such charges are plausible. The problem of waging conventional war in mountainous terrain had previously led the Saleh government to hire thousands of mercenary tribesmen from elsewhere in Yemen to help the army conduct military operations in the north. It is doubtful that these irregulars fight with a great deal of regard for the laws of armed conflict or make a careful effort to distinguish guerrilla fighters from their noncombatant sympathizers. Under these circumstances, the conflict has displaced around 250,000 people, with around 100,000 of these refugees having fled since late 2009 due to an especially intense outbreak of fighting at that time.

The Yemeni government came under considerable international, and especially American, pressure to reach a negotiated solution to the Houthi war in the aftermath of the December 2009 terrorist bombing attempt against a Detroit, Michigan-bound U.S. civilian aircraft by an individual trained by anti-government extremists in Yemen (which will be discussed later).

Many U.S. and allied leaders would prefer to see the Yemeni government concentrate its efforts on defeating al-Qaeda rather than fighting the Houthis, and the failed attack on a U.S. aircraft served to intensify these priorities. The Yemenis have responded to this pressure by stressing that they are already making strong progress against al-Qaeda and have achieved peace with the Houthis. The shaky nature of the current truce nevertheless suggests that cooperative relations will have to be strengthened and consolidated as quickly as possible in order to avoid collapse.

The Southern Movement.

The Yemeni government is also deeply concerned about a serious secessionist movement in the southern part of the country, which reemerged as a significant political force in 2007. Although almost all of the important leaders of the Southern Movement emphatically stress nonviolent political confrontation, the government views them as a grave and potentially expanding threat against Yemeni national unity, fearing they may ultimately shift to routine use of violent tactics. Moreover, the disagreement between the two sides to this conflict could hardly be more fundamental. The unification of the two Yemens is an especially sensitive issue to the Sana'a leadership and is sufficiently weighty to be viewed as the president's most significant achievement in over 30 years of rule. On a more pragmatic level, the Saleh government would be loathe to surrender vital oil producing areas of the Hadhramout area of the south before the resources there have been fully extracted. Perhaps most significantly, a breakaway southern regime could establish itself as an enemy of the current government once it achieved independence. In this regard, the PDRY was often at odds with its northern neighbor during its separate existence, and there were two border wars between the Yemens when they were separate countries, one in 1972 and the other in 1979.[75] An additional concern is that the south itself has serious fissures and that a break with northern Yemen may not result in a unified southern state. Different portions of the southern region may seek independence or quasi-independence, following any break with Sana'a. This possibility is particularly serious with the important Hadhramout province, whose people sometime view themselves as quite distinct from other Yemenis.[76]

The current confrontation between the northern-dominated government and southern secessionists appears to date back to differing expectations about how a unified Yemen would be governed following the 1990 merger. The unification of the two countries was undertaken without a great deal of preparation or transitional moves, despite the vastly different types of governments and political cultures within the two Yemens. The leaders of South Yemen agreed to unify at a time when their country's circumstances were particularly troubling, and they believed that they possessed few acceptable options. The PDRY had been an expensive client of the Soviet Union, which by 1990 was in unmistakable decline and unwilling to further subsidize Marxist regimes in the developing world. Likewise, during its long involvement with leftist radicalism, the PDRY had managed to get itself placed on the U.S. State Department's list of countries supporting terrorism.[77] Consequently, the prospect of a rapprochement with the United States or the conservative Arab states seemed nonexistent without some dramatic change in the way southern Yemen was perceived internationally. Unfortunately for beleaguered southern leaders, the new and significant oil deposits were discovered only after the two Yemens had agreed to unify. These discoveries would probably have caused southerners to entertain second thoughts about the value of the entire enterprise if they had been identified earlier.

Perhaps because of their dire circumstances, the southern leadership was also inclined to believe the Saleh regime's assurances that they would have an important role in determining the future of a united Yemen and that the political system would reflect a modern political outlook. Most doctrinaire Yemeni socialists felt that faster movement towards secularism and a planned economy was more or less inevitable if Yemen was to advance in the political and economic realms, which they assumed was an underlying goal of both northern and southern Yemenis. They also assumed that their political leadership was especially well-prepared to lead the way to such changes. The northern Yemenis, by contrast, tended to view their role as something akin to that of West Germany absorbing East Germany, a neighboring state that no longer possessed much justification for an independent existence after its system of government had failed.[78] The northern leadership further believed that they should have a larger role in deciding their nation's future since the population of the YAR was significantly larger than that of the PDRY. Saleh successfully used the latter argument as the decisive reason for him to retain the presidency after the two countries unified, while the PDRY leader became vice president.

Yemen's unification was accompanied by both sides' acceptance of a variety of democratic institutions and the development of a multiparty political system that was expected to create opportunities for all Yemenis to work through their political and economic differences. Throughout the process, President Saleh nevertheless maintained a disproportionate level of control over the country's finances, while significant steps to unify the separate militaries were never taken due to the distrust of both sides. The Yemeni president used his political power and skills to ensure that he and the GPC were able to marginalize the influence of many of the most important southern leaders, while cultivating pliable figurehead allies from the south. This approach helped bolster the appearance of power-sharing, while actually undermining it. This task became much easier after the GPC won the parliamentary elections in a landslide in April 1993, with the former governing party of South Yemen (Yemeni Socialist Party—YSA) emerging as a distant third behind the GPC and the Islamic party, Islah.[79] As their political setbacks multiplied, many southern leaders came to regret their decision to support the merger. This situation reached a crisis in 1994 as the former leaders of the PDRY attempted to dissolve the union and reestablish a separate southern state after they came to the conclusion that southern interests and their own vision for a united Yemen were being largely ignored. A 10-week civil war followed, in which around 7,000 Yemenis died and the southern secessionists were decisively defeated.[80] Most of their leadership that was able to do so fled into exile to escape charges of treason and probable execution.

Secessionism reemerged as a visible and expanding political force during summer 2007, being touched off by the anger of forcibly retired officers from the PDRY's army and air force. These officers and their supporters became involved in political demonstrations against the extremely low level of support former members of the southern military received in military pensions after quietly seeking redress for a number of years. Predictably, as the forced retirees of a defeated military, they had virtually no influence with which to press the government to move forward on their grievances. Moreover, the government's dismissive treatment of the ex-officers was widely viewed in the south as yet another symbol of a vindictive northern occupation in the aftermath of the 1994 civil war. The impasse also served as a spark unleashing southern anger after a range of other perceived affronts. Most southerners continued to believe that their region suffered widespread neglect while southern leaders were accorded only a cosmetic and stage-managed role in policymaking.

Under these conditions, it is hardly surprising that the secessionist movement continued to grow after being ignited by the retired officers' demonstrations.[81] In December 2007, the full scope of the movement became clear as the result of a massive funeral procession for four southern men killed by security forces under suspicious circumstances. Estimates suggest that hundreds of thousands of mourners attended, thereby demonstrating their solidarity with the southern cause.[82] Enthusiasm for the cause of independence also surged in the aftermath of this event. By 2009, large numbers of protesters were attending recurring rallies, where a number of participants waved the flag of the former Marxist republic.[83] Moreover, there are now at least seven activist organizations seeking southern independence.[84] The Southern Movement has also held rallies at particularly sensitive times, such as directly after Yemeni presidential appeals for increased aid from abroad.[85] The reasoning here is that these rallies may complicate aid requests and perhaps more importantly cause the government to moderate repressive actions while it is appealing for foreign support, at least to the extent of limiting the use of deadly force against demonstrators. The government has responded to increased agitation by raising the visibility of military and security forces on the streets during times of tension and by maintaining rigorous efforts to prevent demonstrations that have been organized without permits.[86]

Activists struggling for southern independence also face the possibility of arrest on such charges as inciting violence and undermining national unity. Sentences for such actions can be quite hefty, as indicated in a March 2010 decision by a special security court to sentence a leading activist of the southern independence struggle to 5 years in prison on these charges.[87] One month later, four activists convicted on similar charges were given 10-year sentences.[88] Many of the prisoners who have received these sentences have so far been defiant. Two of them have stated that they consider the verdict to be a medal which they would wear proudly.[89] At least one of the prisoners has refused to appeal his verdict. There have also been harsh government measures employed to prevent or break up demonstrations, including the use of tear gas and firing live ammunition at or near protestors. The rules of engagement for these encounters are not clear to outsiders, but there have been a number of demonstrations where protestors have been wounded, and a few have been killed in various incidents. As with certain other countries (such as royalist Iran in 1978-79), protestor deaths do not always quell unrest, and in Yemen they sometimes spark new and larger demonstrations in response to the deaths of peaceful activists.[90] The government consistently defends the actions of the security forces and opposes efforts to initiate independent investigations regarding the use of force.[91]

Brutality against demonstrators is inherently dangerous since Yemeni civilians have easy access to firearms, and any use of deadly force against demonstrators can potentially turn into a bloodbath.[92] The vast majority of the Southern Movement has nevertheless remained strongly committed to nonviolence despite the serious and recurring problems at demonstrations. This restraint is especially impressive given the wide variety of loosely coordinated organizations under the umbrella of the Southern Movement, but there are also smaller groups seeking southern independence through the use of violence, and there have been a few instances of rioting as well.[93] On some occasions, individual Yemeni soldiers away from their comrades have been killed in the south, and the Yemeni news media sometimes describe these events as assassinations by secessionists. More recently, government car convoys have been ambushed including two separate motorcades, each carrying a different deputy prime minister. These incidents also led to suspicions toward southern secessionists.[94] That interpretation is nevertheless unproven and probably wrong since al-Qaeda has a strong presence in the south and is deeply desirous of striking at governmental targets. Under these conditions, the mainstream Southern Movement's reputation for nonviolence remains relatively untarnished, at least for the time being.

Despite its regional popularity, the Southern Movement appears to have a number of important weaknesses that limit its ability to challenge the state or even control its supporters. As noted above, the movement is highly diverse. There also appears to be no organizational structures capable of serious coordination among the different groups seeking southern independence. Moreover, most of the organizations within the Southern Movement receive only limited funding and outside assistance from Yemenis working abroad. In particular, Yemeni expatriate sympathizers working in the Gulf are usually blocked from contributing by financial regulations in their host countries. Moreover, support from foreign countries appears nonexistent.[95] While accepting funds from foreign countries is almost always a bad idea, the absence of alternative income has led to a clearly impoverished political movement. Additionally, some leaders of the Southern Movement are reported to be concerned that the government's cease-fire with the Houthis will allow them to move more decisively in repressing the struggle for southern independence.

One of the most prominent Southern Movement leaders to emerge in recent years has been Sheikh Tariq al-Fadhli. Fadhli is an important former ally of President Saleh who participated in the anti-Soviet war in Afghanistan during the 1980s and did not associate himself with the Southern Movement until 2009. He is sometimes described as a former bin Laden associate, and even as an "old friend."[96] Fadhli denies these characterizations, maintaining that while he did meet Osama bin Laden in Afghanistan, they were never close. He also insists that he fought against the Soviets beside local Afghan guerrilla commanders, and not as a bin Laden confidant or subordinate. Fadhli has denounced bin Laden's international terrorist activities, and also stated that Yemen needs a positive relationship with the West.[97] To underscore this point, he had himself videotaped raising an American flag at his family compound in southern Yemen and placed the scene on the Internet.[98] Such antics are difficult to take seriously, and even if Fadhli has given up on jihadist radicalism, he remains an inherently more violence-prone figure than other southern leaders.

While Fadhli's unsavory past may be troubling for many of the Southern Movement's leaders, he is not their most serious public relations headache. The most serious problem developed in May 2009, when Nasser al-Wahayshi, the leader of al-Qaeda's branch in Yemen—al-Qaeda in the Arabian Peninsula (AQAP)—proclaimed his organization's support for southern independence.[99] In the same statement, the al-Qaeda leader sternly warned southerners that Marxism was a failed ideology, and that it could not provide any useful guidelines for achieving their goals. Only jihad could lead them to victory.[100] Wahayshi's support for the south was correspondingly conditional and can be interpreted as a demand for southern acceptance of al-Qaeda leadership for their struggle.

Such demands are disconcerting and repellent to most of the southern leadership at this time, and none of the mainstream groups within the Southern Movement have shown any interest in working with al-Qaeda or adopting its tactics. Instead, they are alarmed about the potential for the government to capitalize on al-Qaeda statements of solidarity to convince the international community that a serious link exists.[101] Such perceptions could be used by the government to justify increased repression in the south with much less fear of an international backlash. Some activists claim that the government is already arresting southern independence supporters on trumped up charges of working with al-Qaeda.[102] Southern Movement leaders may also fear that hotheads in their own organization might eventually be attracted to al-Qaeda if they remain unable to show results for their non-violent efforts.

President Saleh has stated that his government is willing to engage in dialogue with "pro-unity elements [in the south] who have legitimate demands. But we don't have dialogue with separatist elements."[103] This offer is underscored by the government's continued reference to the entire Southern Movement as composed of terrorists or agents of foreign powers.[104] While the president cannot reasonably deny the existence of large anti-government demonstrations in the south, he often claims that the problems bedeviling southerners are more economic than political, and that these problems exist in the north as well. Additionally, any official discussion of casualties at southern rallies inevitably minimizes violence against the demonstrators and instead emphasizes police and security forces casualties.[105]

YEMENI REGIONAL POLITICS AND THE RELATIONSHIP WITH SAUDI ARABIA

Saudi Arabia is Yemen's most important and influential neighbor, and Yemen's future is deeply tied to that of this regional power. The relationship between the two countries is currently strong, although there have been serious tensions between them that have sometimes damaged their bilateral relations. Major events in Yemen almost always have important repercussions in Saudi Arabia, and the Riyadh leadership is deeply aware of this dynamic on issues as diverse as terrorism, the future of Iraq, and even democratic or semi-democratic elections in Yemen. The Saudis sometimes view such elections by neighboring states as a bad example for their own citizens. In this regard, many Saudis seem to view Yemen as a special sphere of influence where Riyadh's concerns trump those of any other outside power. Saudi Arabia has provided subsidies directly to various Yemeni tribes for a number of years without bothering to go through the Sana'a government, thus effectively establishing itself as a separate sovereign capable of providing or withdrawing patronage.[106] Riyadh also supports various religious institutions that favor its version of Islamic orthodoxy. Yemen's desperate need for foreign aid has prevented Sana'a from challenging this sort of meddling. In this regard, Saudi foreign aid has also been provided directly to the government of Yemen and is often more extensive than that provided by any other country. It dwarfs the amounts provided by the United States.[107]

The current close but somewhat uneasy relations between a formal republic and an absolute monarchy have taken a considerable period to forge. After the official end of the North Yemen Civil War in 1970, Sana'a maintained an acceptable relationship with Saudi Arabia until 1990 when Yemen's leadership supported Saddam Hussein in the crisis leading up to the 1991 Gulf War. Although Yemen halfheartedly condemned Iraqi's invasion of Kuwait, it also opposed the anticipated U.S.-led invasion to liberate that country. At that time, Yemen was a nonpermanent member of the United Nations Security Council (UNSC), and its diplomatic actions assumed an importance and level of visibility that was exceptional for the Sana'a government. As the only Arab country then serving on the UNSC, Yemen resisted calls for the use of force against Iraq, called for an undefined "Arab solution" to the conflict, and condemned Saudi Arabia for inviting foreign troops into the kingdom.[108] Most, if not virtually all, of Yemen's government leaders and members of the public were solidly opposed to a UN resolution calling for "all necessary means" to oust Saddam from Kuwait. Many Yemeni officers admired Saddam Hussein, and those who had undergone military training in Iraq were often especially opposed to the potential invasion.[109] President Saleh found such sentiment extremely difficult to ignore, and attempted to avoid offending domestic public opinion by tilting toward Iraq. Moreover, on a geostrategic level, the Saleh government worried that a defeated Iraq would leave Saudi Arabia disproportionately powerful on the Arabian Peninsula, and that such a development could allow the Saudis to dominate Yemen on its key domestic and foreign policies. The Yemeni president apparently believed that he could maintain a good deal more autonomy by maneuvering between the two major Gulf Arab powers rather than by attempting to convince one dominant regional state of the need to help him address Yemen's problems.

Riyadh viewed Yemen's pro-Saddam policies as a betrayal even prior to the UNSC vote authorizing the use of force against Iraq. Many Saudis believed that they had been extremely generous with Yemen, and that Sana'a's support of their enemies at a time of crisis required punishment. On September 19, 1990, Riyadh acted on this anger, revoking the special status of Yemenis allowed to work within Saudi Arabia.[110] This change led to the expulsion of hundreds of thousands of Yemenis from the kingdom, forcing their return to Yemen. Various other Gulf monarchies followed the Saudi example, with many expelling their Yemeni workers to please Riyadh and because they were also angry that Yemen appeared to be siding with an expansionist Iraq. The Yemeni government then made matters worse for itself internationally by voting with Cuba against UNSC Resolution 678, which authorized the U.S.-led coalition to use "all necessary means" to remove Saddam Hussein from Kuwait.[111] This UNSC resolution passed despite Yemeni opposition, and Saddam's value as a regional ally evaporated after Iraq's massive defeat in early 1991. By 1991 over 800,000 Yemenis had returned home after losing their jobs abroad.[112] This setback deeply crippled the always troubled Yemeni economy. Remittances sent by workers to their families in Yemen had previously brought at least one billion dollars per year into the country throughout much of the 1980s, but now dried up.[113] In Yemen, food prices quadrupled, and unemployment reached around 35 percent, thus ensuring that virtually every Yemeni household was hurt by the disaster.[114]

The leadership of Saudi Arabia, Kuwait, and the other Gulf Cooperation Council (GCC) states remained hostile towards Yemen in the years immediately following Operation DESERT STORM. When asked about President Saleh in 1994, the Kuwaiti Foreign Minister bluntly stated, "He is another Saddam Hussein."[115] This was an overstatement, of course, but one that clearly reflected the sense of betrayal some of the Gulf Arabs felt. Although Saudi support may have been mostly rhetorical, they took the surprising step of siding with the southern Yemeni secessionists in the 1994 civil war despite the Marxist orientation of many of their leaders. Publicly, the Saudis and their Arab allies supported a UN call for a Yemeni ceasefire and a mediated end to the conflict, policies which could be expected to head off an impending northern military victory.[116] Riyadh may have also surreptitiously provided more tangible forms of support including weapons and funding, but little evidence exists of such actions. According to a leading scholar of the region, a number of the Gulf monarchies, including Saudi Arabia, allocated funds for weapons and other material support for the southern secessionists, but failed to provide this support to the rebels before their resistance collapsed.[117] The primary Saudi motivation for providing even limited support for the south seems to have been a desire to continue punishing President Saleh for his 1990-91 actions and perhaps to support the division and hence weakening of a potential regional adversary. The Saudis may also have reacted angrily to Saddam Hussein's strong rhetorical support for Saleh's efforts to maintain the Yemeni union by force.[118] Riyadh's policies had little, if any, impact of the outcome of the war since it apparently failed to provide weapons.

Saleh's continuing ability to remain in power following the 1991 war eventually caused the Gulf Arab monarchies to moderate their position of unrelenting hostility toward Sana'a. One key reason for this change was that the Saudis, and especially the Kuwaitis, by the mid-1990s were willing to engage in limited outreach to Arab states that had tilted towards Iraq during the 1990-91 crisis and war.[119] This approach was implemented in the hope of permanently realigning them away from Ba'athist Iraq. By this time, the Gulf leaders understood that Saddam Hussein remained entrenched as Iraq's dictator despite his 1991 defeat, and that he was therefore unlikely to be overthrown by Iraqi moderates seeking better relations with other regional states. Thus, the leaders of the Gulf Arab monarchies sought to ensure that Iraq was isolated from potential sources of political support in any future conflict. That concern meant that relations with Yemen had to be placed on a more normal footing. Aid links were slowly expanded and efforts were made to move forward on bilateral problems.

A number of Yemeni workers were able to return to Saudi Arabia in the second half of the 1990s, and by 2000 some estimates reached as high as 500,000.[120] This number included Yemenis who made special arrangements with Saudi authorities to return, as well as some who were exempted from deportation or had otherwise evaded the requirement to leave Saudi Arabia. This number does not seem to have expanded dramatically since that time as most Yemenis remained confined to unskilled jobs, especially in the construction sector, and minor shopkeeping under the sponsorship of a Saudi citizen. As Saudi Arabia's labor needs have evolved and a more sophisticated workforce has become important, poorly-educated Yemenis have had less to offer.[121] Their most important asset for future work is that they are willing to do hard manual labor that is of no interest to Saudis, although fewer of these jobs are available than in the past. In recent years, the Saudi leadership may also have become concerned about the dangers of increasing numbers of Yemenis in the kingdom for security reasons.[122] The limitations on Yemeni workers allowed to enter Saudi Arabia remain a source of disagreement between the two countries.

A key turning point in improved Saudi-Yemeni relations was seen at the 10-year anniversary celebration of Yemeni unity in May 2000. Saudi Crown Prince (now King) Abdullah attended the event, and thereby became the first Saudi leader to be present at such a function.[123] This action also signaled Riyadh's acceptance of the unification of the two countries which it had previously opposed. Another fairly solid indication of the improvement in Saudi-Yemeni relations took place shortly afterwards on June 12, 2000, when the leaders of the two countries signed a bilateral treaty in Jeddah, Saudi Arabia, on international land and sea borders, expanding upon the Taif Treaty of 1934.[124] The Jeddah Treaty was announced on the first full day of an official visit by President Saleh to Saudi Arabia. As such, it indicated a significant improvement in Saudi-Yemeni relations, and it also dramatically reduced the danger of future confrontations along the border. As late as 1997, border skirmishes had occurred between the two states with Saudi and Yemeni solders engaging in armed conflict. In December 1997 several soldiers died in such a confrontation.[125]

Relations between the two states have continued to improve at a steady pace since the signing of the Jeddah Treaty in 2000. The Saudis have been one of Yemen's most generous aid donors since at least 2006 when they pledged $1 billion dollars in aid, and Saudi Arabia, as noted, is currently Yemen's largest regional supplier of aid.[126] Additionally, Saudi Arabia's GCC partners also provide smaller, but still significant, levels of aid to Yemen. In March 2010, this trend was especially clear at a "Friends of Yemen" conference in Dubai where the GCC states pledged to provide the Yemenis with at least $3.7 billion in aid.[127] Even in this environment, however, tensions can persist, and some Yemenis suspect that the Saudi leadership would like to maintain a status quo whereby Yemen is weak, impoverished, and dependent upon Saudi largess.[128] Such weakness would allow the Saudis to dominate Yemeni politics on issues of importance to the Saudis. While there may be some truth to this argument, Yemen is hardly in a good situation to refuse support from any friendly country, even if Riyadh, with its own agenda, can be somewhat overbearing and intrusive at times.

Along with the provision of foreign aid, the Saudi leadership maintains an especially watchful eye on Yemeni efforts to deal with various national security problems that could expand to include their own country. The example of the Houthi rebellion is especially notable, since Saudi Arabia became embroiled in large-scale combat operations in Yemen against the Houthis on the side of the Sana'a government in 2009. One author suggests that President Saleh manipulated Saudi fears of Shi'ite empowerment to gain Riyadh's support for his own conflict with the Houthis, which may not have required such an overwhelming Saudi response to protect its interests.[129]

There may be some truth to this charge, but Riyadh does not have to be pushed particularly strongly to become concerned over Shi'ite political assertiveness. Saudi fears entail not only their deep disapproval of Shi'ite religious doctrine but also involve the recently intensified Saudi rivalry with Iran.[130] Iran's increased political role in the Gulf since 2003 is often viewed throughout the region as a reflection of Tehran's power-based ascendancy.[131] In some of its worst nightmares, Riyadh worries about Iran and a Shi'ite-dominated Iraq collaborating again in future conflict involving political subversion and proxy struggles. Yemeni government accusations, if perceived as credible, that the Houthis seek to restore a Shi'ite imamate with strong ties to Iran would consequently be of the utmost concern to the Saudi leadership. Such charges may even raise Saudi fears of encirclement by radical Shi'ite enemies. Moreover, official charges of Iranian involvement with the Houthis have been unrelenting.[132] For its part, Tehran denies providing material support to the rebels, and Sana'a has not been able to produce evidence that clearly substantiates its accusations.

There is also the problem of al-Qaeda. From 2003 until 2009, the Saudis fought a prolonged and bloody war with the local branch of the AQAP. Many of the small arms and explosives used by the terrorists in this campaign were smuggled from Yemen, where military grade weapons are seldom difficult to obtain.[133] Saudi coordination with Yemeni officials was therefore useful in the development of anti-terrorism strategies. Such coordination was to become even more important after January 2009, when the Yemeni branch of al-Qaeda announced major structural changes as a result of the al-Qaeda organization's defeat within Saudi Arabia by that country's security forces.

At that time, the Saudi organization and Yemen's al-Qaeda in the Southern Arabian Peninsula (AQSAP) merged into one organization which retained the Saudi name of al-Qaeda in the Arabian Peninsula. AQAP fighters remaining in the kingdom were advised to flee and regroup in Yemen on the understanding that al-Qaeda military operations against the Saudi government would continue from there. This message may have simply formalized a trend which had already been occurring since 2007, when increasing numbers of Saudi jihadists found it sensible to flee their homeland for Yemen.[134] The merger of the two branches of al-Qaeda led to a reinvigoration of the terrorist organization in Yemen, even while the al-Qaeda movement accepted the weakening of its presence in Saudi Arabia (which they viewed as temporary). The merger also raised the possibility that Saudi radicals with strong fundraising skills would help obtain significant additional resources for the newly merged movement at levels that would have stunned the Yemenis in the organization.[135]

The leader (emir) of the new al-Qaeda branch organization was Nasser al-Wahayshi, a Yemeni and past junior aide to bin Laden in Afghanistan.[136] A former Guantanamo prisoner and Saudi national, Saeed al-Shihri became the deputy leader of AQAP. Al-Shihri had been released from Guantanamo Bay in 2007 and was placed in the Saudi rehabilitation program, becoming one of the most high-profile failures associated with that program.[137] Both of these men were determined to continue the struggle against the Saudi monarchy, despite the fact that the new organization was now based in Yemen. Typically, they managed to express this strategy in an insulting and condescending way when in August 2009, an AQAP internet publication stated, "We concentrate on Saudi Arabia because the government of Ali Abdullah Saleh is on the verge of collapse [and he is about to] flee the land of Yemen."[138]

It would have perhaps been more accurate to state that Saudi Arabia is a much larger prize for al-Qaeda than Yemen, and victory in Saudi Arabia could be followed by success throughout the Gulf. Moreover, it is also untrue to suggest that al-Qaeda was not interested in undertaking terrorist strikes against Yemen. Rather, they were interested in mounting operations against both Saudi and Yemeni governmental targets as subsequent events ultimately proved. AQAP is nevertheless correct in indicating that the Saleh regime is facing a variety of serious challenges, and that its survival is by no means assured.

Despite the destruction of al-Qaeda's power base in Saudi Arabia, AQAP mounted an extremely ambitious, but ultimately unsuccessful operation against the Saudi royal family from Yemen in August 2009, when they attempted to assassinate Prince Moham-mad bin Nayef. Prince Mohammad is the son of the current Saudi Interior Minister and holds the key po-sition of Director of Counterterrorism within the Min-istry of Interior. As such, he is an important emerging leader of Saudi Arabia's next generation of leaders, as well as a direct and active adversary of al-Qaeda. The assassination attempt was well planned and profes-sional. It involved a meeting between Prince Moham-med and Abdullah Hassan Tali al-Asiri, a supposedly repentant 23-year-old militant who maintained that he wanted to present the prince with a list of al-Qaeda members in Yemen who wished to surrender and en-ter the Saudi rehabilitation program. Shortly after he entered Prince Mohammed's presence, al-Asiri set off a concealed bomb.[139] Prince Mohammed was not seri-ously injured in the effort, although his assailant was killed instantly. A great deal of luck was apparent in this outcome since virtually identical tactics led to the deaths of seven Central Intelligence Agency (CIA) of-ficials and one Jordanian intelligence officer in Khost, Afghanistan, on December 30, 2009.

THE ORIGINS AND DEVELOPMENT OF THE Al-QAEDA PRESENCE IN YEMEN

Osama bin Laden was born a Saudi citizen, al-though his father, Mohammed bin Laden, was born in the village of al-Rubat in the southern Yemeni province of Hadhramaut. This area is often described as bin Laden's ancestral home.[140] The younger bin Laden's affinity for Yemen appears to have remained strong throughout his career as the leader of al-Qaeda. In the past, bin Laden has employed Yemeni jihadists in a variety of positions of special trust including his personal bodyguards, drivers, and other aides.[141] The youngest of bin Laden's wives is also a Yemeni from the southern highlands of that country. Little is known about her, but she became bin Laden's fourth wife at between 15 to 18 years of age sometime in 2000 about a year before the September 11, 2001 (9/11) strikes.[142] Bin Laden married her after agreeing to a divorce requested by one of his other wives.[143] He did not select the young bride himself but instead sent a Yemeni aide to the Hadhramaut to find someone appropriate. It is likely that bin Laden sought a Yemeni as his new fourth wife in the hopes of establishing kinship ties that could benefit him in reaching out to important tribal and religious figures in Yemen.[144] Various other al-Qaeda members are reported to have married Yemenis from Marib, al-Jawf, and Shabwa governorates, where al-Qaeda has been especially interested in establishing a meaningful presence.[145]

It nevertheless appears that bin Laden has been largely unsuccessful in using these marriage ties (as well as his wealth and largess) to reach out to Yemen tribal leaders for tangible support beyond the sheltering of some jihadist subordinates and allies.[146] Certainly, he had received significantly less such support than he sought from Yemeni tribal leaders whom he may have hoped would help overthrow President Saleh and replace him with a government allied with al-Qaeda (such as the Taliban government in pre-9/11 Afghanistan). Unfortunately for bin Laden, important Yemeni tribal leaders have never been interested in confronting the Saleh government for his sake or that of his movement. Conversely, they are sometimes willing to perform some services for al-Qaeda, including sheltering terrorists, in exchange for funds. In these instances, the motivations for helping bin Laden seem to have be almost entirely financial, and not ideological.[147]

Relations between bin Laden and the Yemeni government (like those between bin Laden and the Saudi government) found a solid basis for cooperation during the 1980s before the international jihadist movement rose to prominence. During President Saleh's early years as the leader of North Yemen, bin Laden had not yet publicly embraced the theories of global revolution and a restored Islamic caliphate that were later to dominate his thinking and behavior, though both men were concerned about the Soviet invasion of Afghanistan. During the anti-Soviet guerrilla war in Afghanistan (1979-88), the Yemeni government cooperated with bin Laden's representatives who helped recruit young men to travel to Afghanistan and participate in that struggle.[148]

Yemen's government considered fighting against Soviet troops occupying a Muslim country to be an honorable and natural course for those youths, many of whom had few other viable opportunities at home. In this supportive political environment, Yemen provided more Arab fighters to the struggle against the Soviets in Afghanistan than did any other country except Saudi Arabia, and the Yemeni combatants were much tougher than the Saudis.[149] Yemeni fighters participating in the conflict may have numbered in the tens of thousands.[150] While most of the Arab international forces were not particularly effective in waging war against Soviet troops (especially when compared to indigenous Afghan fighters), Yemeni fighters did nevertheless undergo military training and participated in a variety of skirmishes and a few battles. These often poorly educated individuals also received extensive political indoctrination, as well as the opportunity to associate with radicals from many other countries. Politically, Yemeni fighters were among bin Laden's most committed supporters recruited for service in the anti-Soviet jihad in Afghanistan.

Another key reason bin Laden was able to recruit so many Yemenis was his skillful effort to reach out to youths from former landowning families who had fled from the Marxist PDRY regime and established a marginal existence in either North Yemen or Saudi Arabia.[151] Because of their own searing experiences in southern Yemen, many of these aggrieved young men were receptive to recruitment by any Islamist organization opposed to secularism and communism. Upon coming to power, the PDRY government had adapted an orthodox communist attitude toward religion as a fraudulent and anti-modern force. This worldview led to intermittent government persecution of Islamic figures and the destruction of religious sites, especially in the early 1970s. At the height of this persecution, the graves of prominent theologians (sometimes carelessly described as "Islamic saints") were desecrated, and some clerics and Islamic scholars were murdered.[152] Conservative young men who fled South Yemen to serve later in al-Qaeda therefore directed their fierce anti-communism and religious devotion to serve bin Laden's objectives. They also viewed the bin Laden family's roots in southern Yemen with great favor. Many Yemeni recruits further hoped that the war in Afghanistan would be preliminary to an effort to retake their homeland in South Yemen.

Bin Laden probably encouraged followers to view South Yemen as a likely center of future guerrilla operations. After the Soviet withdrawal from Afghanistan allowed him to focus elsewhere, bin Laden displayed much interest in ousting the PDRY's Marxist government and replacing it with his version of an Islamist government.[153] He may even have promised his Yemeni subordinates that he would make military operations within South Yemen a priority upon the defeat of the Soviets in Afghanistan. Such a promise would have been sincere. Following the Soviet withdrawal from Afghanistan, the future terrorist leader was looking for new heroic struggles and had no desire to fade away quietly as a nonentity in his family's construction business. Moreover, in August 1988, he and other like-minded leaders formed al-Qaeda, although the organization's more sweeping purposes, and even its name, were then enshrouded in secrecy.[154] At this time, bin Laden may have believed that his forces played a major military role in defeating the Soviets in Afghanistan, although more objective analysis suggests that the combat activities of these forces had little real impact on the outcome of the war.[155] Such beliefs would have fed his dreams of playing a major role on the world stage with the destruction of the Arab World's only communist regime serving as an ideal stepping stone to larger concerns. In line with such thinking, in 1989 bin Laden approached Prince Turki al-Feisal, the head of Saudi intelligence, offering to lead and help fund a new struggle against the PDRY in cooperation with the Saudi intelligence services.[156] The Riyadh leadership, which detested the PDRY and did not yet consider bin Laden a criminal, may have seriously considered the offer but ultimately decided against such an effort. Saudi leaders had already come to believe that bin Laden was difficult to control and may not have favored the idea of a private guerrilla army operating outside of their direct control in Yemen.[157]

Bin Laden found the Saudi royal family's response to his offer on South Yemen to be a bitter disappointment, but this was not to be his most serious disagreement with the leadership. Instead, the estrangement reached a breaking point in 1990 when the Riyadh government allowed U.S. troops to be stationed in their country as a response to the Iraqi invasion of Kuwait. Bin Laden began openly and fiercely criticizing the Saudi government and was allowed to go into exile in Sudan in 1992. At this time, he became increasingly comfortable operating behind the backs of Saudi security officials, and in 1994 his Saudi citizenship was revoked for funding subversive activities in several Arab countries, including Egypt and Yemen. Previously, around the time of Yemeni unification in 1990, bin Laden had helped to fund a terrorist training facility in southern Yemen's Abayan province in apparent defiance of Prince Turki's instructions.[158] Bin Laden disapproved of Yemeni unification because of the initial inclusion of a number of southern communists in high government posts. After unification, a campaign of assassination took place in the south in which some 100 officials with ties to the Yemeni Socialist Party were killed or wounded. While the identities of the assassins were uncertain for some time, it later became clear that the killers were jihadists returned from Afghanistan, at least some of whom were probably associated with bin Laden.[159]

Throughout the early 1990s, President Saleh's government generally viewed Yemeni jihadists returning from Afghanistan 1990s as brave and honorable men who were not to be subjected to any special scrutiny or surveillance as occurred in other Arab nations such as Jordan.[160] Abu Musab al-Suri, a leading al-Qaeda military theorist and intellectual, even went so far as to refer to Yemen as a "safe haven" for jihadis in the years immediately following the Soviet-Afghan war.[161] After Yemeni unification in May 1990, President Saleh also viewed the Islamist Afghan war veterans as a useful political counterweight to southern Marxists in his policies of playing off conflicting groups against each other to remain in power. The value of these veterans to the Yemeni government later increased when up to three brigades of Yemeni jihadists were employed as auxiliaries of the Yemeni army during the 1994 civil war. This force made an important contribution to the rapid northern victory against southern secessionists, and many of the jihadists were rewarded with military, security, and other government jobs after the war ended.[162] Others left Yemen and volunteered for service to al-Qaeda in the Afghan civil war on the side of the Taliban.[163]

Other jihadists and Afghanistan veterans did not leave Yemen and refused to be co-opted by the Yemeni government. These individuals engaged in activities within Yemen that were to become the seeds of serious problems later. Such actions included making plans to undertake terrorist activities against Western targets. Al-Qaeda is believed to have maintained a meaningful presence in Yemen since at least the early 1990s. The first al-Qaeda terrorist attack against Westerners may have been a coordinated strike at two hotels in Aden, Yemen, in 1992. These attacks appear to have been aimed at killing American soldiers travelling to their duty station in Somalia, but instead killed an Australian tourist and two Yemenis.[164]

In the strike, al-Qaeda seems to have been coordinating with an organization known as the Aden-Abyan Islamic Army (AAIA). The AAIA was led by Abu Hassan al-Mihdar, a Yemeni veteran of the Soviet-Afghan War, and its leadership shared many al Qaeda values and goals including, and most especially, its opposition to U.S. influence in the region.[165] The

AAIA set up at least one training camp in southern Yemen, and in 1998 kidnapped 16 Western hostages, four of whom were killed in a shootout between the AAIA and the Yemeni army.[166] AAIA may have taken the lead in this attack, with al-Qaeda's endorsement. Cable News Network (CNN) reporter Peter Bergen, who researched bin Laden's activities in Yemen well before 9/11, suggests that Tariq al-Fadhli may have been al-Qaeda's senior man in Yemen at this time and could also have been involved in the strikes.[167]

Al-Qaeda's Yemen-based operatives appear to have provided some support for the August 7, 1998, terrorist bombings of the U.S. embassies in Kenya and Tanzania, although no Yemenis directly participated in the attacks.[168] Some studies suggest that the AAIA may have cooperated with al-Qaeda in the attack on the USS *Cole* in October 12, 2000, noting that the strike may have been designed to coincide roughly with the execution of a captured AAIA leader by the Yemeni government.[169] Even if this is true, al-Qaeda dominated the attack on the U.S. warship, and bin Laden personally supervised the assault, including the choice of target, selection of the operatives, funding of expenses, and overruling of local recommendations.[170] Local operatives initially envisioned the attack as using an explosives-laden boat to attack a commercial ship in Aden harbor. Viewing such a plan as too timid, bin Laden directed them to strike against an American warship, which ultimately was the destroyer, USS *Cole*. While the *Cole* was not sunk in the attack, it did have a large hole torn open on one side, with 17 sailors killed and 40 wounded. The AAIA, for its part, continues to exist and is usually considered to be al-Qaeda affiliated, although its importance has been almost totally overshadowed by al-Qaeda.[171] Both groups were viewed as problems by the Yemeni government in the aftermath of this event, but not major security threats.

While the embassy bombings and the *Cole* attack were important, al-Qaeda's strikes against the twin towers and the Pentagon on 9/11 were dramatically more significant. No Yemeni citizens directly participated in the 9/11 strikes against the United States, despite their importance within al-Qaeda strategy, but this was not because of a lack of trust on bin Laden's part for his Yemeni subordinates. Rather, the terrorist leader considered Yemenis travelling on their country's passports to be a poor choice for service in terrorist strikes against New York and Washington. Bin Laden feared that individuals with Yemeni passports would stand out in any U.S. security screening process in ways that Arabs from countries more closely aligned with the United States would not. Nevertheless, there was a more subtle Yemeni link in these operations since Saudis of Yemeni descent filled at least five of the "muscle" hijackers positions in the 9/11 attacks.[172] These individuals often came from areas within Saudi Arabia that were more culturally akin to Yemen than Riyadh. The choice of such people for hijacking roles may have reflected a bin Laden belief that al-Qaeda members of Yemeni heritage are often more suited to tasks involving force and intimidation than other Saudi Arabians.

The 9/11 strikes changed everything about how the Yemeni government viewed al-Qaeda. Whereas prior to the attacks President Saleh seemed to consider them one more distasteful faction to be manipulated and played against other enemies, they had now become instigators of a major crisis that required a fundamental reexamination of key Yemeni foreign and domestic policies.[173] Saleh understood the dangers for his regime presented by the 9/11 strikes and was concerned about the "with us or against us" rhetoric of the Bush administration. Yemen's reputation of laxity with Islamic militants and earlier U.S. disappointment over the level of cooperation on the USS *Cole* investigation suggested the possibility of serious emerging problems with the United States unless the government generated some newfound support for the U.S.-declared war on terrorism. Consequently, Saleh opted for a more unambiguous alignment with Washington in the struggle against al-Qaeda. In January 2002, around 600 potentially dangerous foreigners studying Islam at Yemeni institutions were deported.[174] Even more significantly, in 2002 six al-Qaeda terrorists, including several key leaders in Marib, Yemen, were killed in what the Yemeni government has now admitted to have been an authorized U.S. Predator drone attack.[175] Among the dead was Qaid Sinan al-Harithi, the head of the al-Qaeda branch, then known as al-Qaeda in Yemen. According to journalistic sources, the strike was expected to remain a secret, but broad hints of U.S. involvement made by a senior U.S. official during a CNN interview caused the cover story to collapse.[176] The U.S.-Yemeni struggle against al-Qaeda nevertheless continued, and in November 2003, Yemeni security forces captured Muhammed al-Ahdal, who was then al-Harithi's replacement as the head of al-Qaeda in Yemen.[177] In 2004, with the al-Qaeda problem seemingly minimized and contained, the Yemeni government became much more focused on its conflict with the Houthis, while Washington directed its attention at problems associated with managing violence in post-Saddam Iraq.

Yemeni jihadists also directed at least some of their attention to Iraq shortly after the 2003 invasion. The number of Yemenis who fought in Iraq as supporters of al-Qaeda after the 2003 U.S.-led invasion of that country is uncertain, but many Yemenis were given ample opportunity to fight in that country if they wished to do so. In the initial stages of the Iraq War, when public fury over the invasion was still white hot, Yemen's government maintained a tolerant approach to militants going to Iraq, doing little to prevent them from leaving for Iraq while not punishing them upon their return. The Yemeni government also did not prevent various radical clerics, including the very prominent Sheikh Abdul Majeed al-Zindani, from openly encouraging young men to travel to Iraq to join the fighting.[178]

Additionally, the activist Islamist organization, *al-Hikma al-Yemania*, was reported to have helped recruit and transport would-be fighters, although this organization strongly denies any links to al-Qaeda or involvement in supplying recruits to fight in the Iraq War.[179] Cell phone videos of al-Qaeda units fighting in Iraq have been reported to be an important recruiting tool for al-Qaeda cells in Yemen.[180] Some estimates state that as many as 2,000 Yemeni fighters participated in the fighting for the first 7 years of the war, but this figure seems high, considering that the total number of non-Iraqi jihadists was seldom more than 300 at any one time, according to most reliable estimates.[181] The Sinjar documents captured by U.S. forces in Iraq (the so-called "al-Qaeda rolodex," which discusses only a portion of foreign jihadi activities within a limited timeframe) mention 48 Yemenis who crossed into Iraq from Syria near the area where the documents were seized.[182]

THE INTENSIFICATION AND EXPANSION OF THE Al-QAEDA THREAT IN YEMEN

The al-Qaeda threat within Yemen seems to have revived and intensified around 2006. One of the reasons frequently given for this change is that a group of 23 experienced and resourceful terrorists escaped *en mass* from a Yemeni Political Security Organization (PSO) prison in February 2006. The escape of these individuals appeared suspiciously easy, and skeptics have suggested that the escape might have been facilitated by jihadist sympathizers within the PSO, or even at the higher levels of the government. Such a search for blame was probably inevitable, since the 2006 prison break has often been treated as an event of seismic proportions for the revitalization of al-Qaeda in Yemen. The importance given to this event is nevertheless surprising, owing to the limited number of individuals involved in the escape. Moreover, not all of these individuals had much of a chance to cause additional trouble after they escaped. Within about a year of the prison break, six of them were dead, and 11 had been returned to custody. Only six of the former prisoners remained at large in Yemen.[183] Consequently, there remains a clear need to look for additional factors in al-Qaeda's revitalization within Yemen.

Perhaps of greater importance than the 2006 prison break in al-Qaeda's revitalization were the developments in neighboring Saudi Arabia in the late 2000s. By 2007, a number of Saudi terrorists were making their way to Yemen, bringing much better financed terrorists into contact with the Yemenis. The announced merger of the Saudi and Yemeni branches of al-Qaeda in January 2009 was naturally of the greatest concern to the Sana'a government, underscoring the danger presented by strongly revitalized al-Qaeda forces in Yemen. Yemeni authorities responded to this new threat as best they could in the weeks immediately following this declaration when the security forces rounded up 170 al-Qaeda suspects and other bad risks. These individuals were forced to sign pledges that they would not engage in terrorism and then released to the supervision of their tribal leaders.[184] While the pledges themselves cannot be viewed as a serious deterrent, they were an unmistakable warning to these individuals that they were under suspicion and could find themselves facing long terms of imprisonment (if not a death sentence) for future misbehavior. Likewise, the tribal leaders involved in this situation are required to guarantee the good behavior of individuals as a condition of their release into tribal custody. Such actions may therefore have some value in preventing various radicals and malcontents from drifting into al-Qaeda activities, but are probably of limited effectiveness in influencing the activities of hard-core terrorists.

Yemeni radicals may have been able, in part, to rebuild their organization because in contrast to their behavior in Saudi Arabia, the al-Qaeda forces in Yemen do not have a history of striking at civilians within their own society, so long as those civilians are outside of the government (although some have been killed in crossfire or died in strikes on oil infrastructure). Rather, al-Qaeda operations in Yemen are aimed at the security forces and at foreign targets such as the U.S. embassy, which was struck by mortar shells in March 2008. In this instance, the shells fell short of the embassy, but killed a guard and injured 13 students at a nearby girl's school.[185] Two al-Qaeda members were later apprehended and sentenced to death for this action.[186] A larger and much better planned attack occurred on September 16, 2008, when six al-Qaeda operatives disguised as police officers attacked the embassy with car bombs, killing 16 people, including one American. Another serious attack against the Western diplomatic presence in Yemen occurred in April 2010 when an al-Qaeda suicide bomber attempted to kill the British ambassador by targeting his car convoy in Sana'a. The ambassador was unhurt, although three bystanders were wounded and the bomber killed.[187] The attempted assassination of a well-protected British diplomat is more an embarrassment for the Yemeni government than a crisis, since no United Kingdom (UK) nationals were seriously injured or killed. But it strikes once again at one of Yemen's only promising sources of future revenue, tourism, hurting the government without striking directly at the population. It is doubtful that average Yemenis, with their own problems, give much thought to such strikes.

There are also questions about the role that returning Yemeni jihadists from Iraq might have had on al-Qaeda's revitalization in Yemen. A *Newsweek* journalist, quoting unnamed sources, stated in 2008 that returning fighters from Iraq had brought important military and planning experience to al-Qaeda forces in Yemen, and that their activities have been of intense concern to the Yemeni government.[188] These returning radicals have been described as skilled at avoiding surveillance and detection by the security police and experienced enough in countersurveillance procedures to avoid obvious mistakes such as the use of cell phones and emails. Additional journalistic sources suggest that the car-bombing techniques used in the September 2008 attack on the U.S. embassy represent a new level of sophistication for Yemeni terrorists and that such skills were probably learned in Iraq or Somalia rather than from the Internet.[189] Yemeni security officials later confirmed this, stating that several of the captured attackers involved in the assault had fought in Iraq.[190] Such assessments appear reasonable since al-Qaeda in Iraq was experiencing severe setbacks by 2007. According to the former head of the bin Laden assessments desk at the CIA, al-Qaeda in Iraq specifically called upon al-Qaeda forces in Yemen to provide more fighters to support the struggling Iraqi radicals.[191] Such fighters were quickly promised as an act of solidarity, but it is not known how seriously Yemeni al-Qaeda members followed up on this request. There also appear to have been a number of important internal changes taking place in al-Qaeda's Yemeni branch as younger and more radical members of the organization, hardened by fighting in Iraq and elsewhere, demanded that their leadership challenge the Saleh government more directly.[192] These younger fighters were infuriated by the invasion of Iraq to a degree that did not occur with most older leaders. They were also much less forgiving towards Saleh's cooperation with the United States than their elders and, in many cases, sought confrontation with the Yemeni government.[193] Additionally, as the U.S. military presence in Iraq continued, many Yemenis believed, or at least did not discount, al-Qaeda propaganda about continuing American atrocities committed against innocent Iraqi civilians, thereby strengthening the radicals.

As noted earlier, one of the most well-known al-Qaeda operations took place on December 25, 2009, when an operative trained in Yemen attempted to blow up a Northwest Airline passenger jet with 280 people aboard. In response, Yemen quickly announced that it has arrested 29 people believed to be members of al-Qaeda in a domestic crackdown on that organization.[194] While it is doubtful that bin Laden or any of his closest aides knew about the Christmas bombing, the al-Qaeda leader's endorsement of this operation may help AQAP's current leadership support their legitimacy within jihadist circles in Yemen.[195] President Obama responded to the bombing attempt by announcing a number of concerns about U.S. intelligence procedures that had failed in this instance, stating that the United States would begin pursuing solutions to these difficulties. He also announced plans to expand efforts to help the Yemeni government implement an effective counterterrorism program. The President further maintained that he had "no intention of sending U.S. boots on the ground" to Yemen (or Somalia) as a result of this incident. He stated that "in countries like Yemen, in countries like Somalia, I think working with international partners is most effective at this point."[196] President Obama's statement echoed earlier remarks by U.S. military leaders, including Admiral Mike Mullen, Chairman of the Joint Chiefs of Staff, who asserted that sending U.S. combat troops to Yemen was "not a possibility."[197] Yet, these statements were apparently not unequivocal enough for some important Yemeni political figures, who noted that the American political leader did not maintain that the United States would never send troops to Yemen under any circumstances. Radical Sheikh Abdul Majeed Zindani was particularly incensed, suggesting that the U.S. leader had left the door open to possible military intervention in the future as part of an elaborate conspiracy to declare Yemen a failing state and then to seize its oil facilities, thus allowing "the return of colonialism."[198]

As the struggle against al-Qaeda escalated, Sana'a lost its reputation for lenient treatment of radicals and become more willing to work with the United States. A December 24, 2009, air strike was widely described in the press as a U.S. Navy cruise missile attack authorized by the Yemeni government to target regional al-Qaeda leaders.[199] The government of Yemen acknowledged an air strike but did not elaborate. Unfortunately, key al-Qaeda leaders appear to have evaded or survived the attack. Yemen again intensified its military operations against al-Qaeda in the aftermath of the Christmas 2009 failed terrorist bombing, when President Saleh expressed concern about more U.S. criticism of his inability to control terrorist actions originating in his country. According to *New York Times* journalist Robert Worth, Saleh was presented with "irrefutable evidence" in the fall of 2010 that AQAP was seeking to destroy the regime by assassinating him and his relatives.[200] Worth maintains that this development caused the Yemeni government to move much more aggressively against al-Qaeda forces.[201] AQAP has responded to government operations with its own efforts to retaliate against the Saleh government. Another audacious al-Qaeda operation occurred on July 15, 2010, when approximately 20 al-Qaeda gunmen attacked the intelligence and security headquarters in Zinjibar, the capital of the often restive Abayan province.[202] Three police officers were killed in this hit-and-run attack, and 11 were wounded. Two AQAP members were also killed and one wounded.

There are also emerging signs that AQAP operations against the government may be taking on a new and more virulent form. In this regard, al-Qaeda has sought to use the confrontation between the Yemeni government and the Southern Movement to its advantage if at all possible. In mid-2010, AQAP launched several high profile attacks against important government targets in southern Yemen, causing a number of government casualties and probably embarrassing the security forces.[203] These attacks led to intensive government efforts to root out al-Qaeda forces in Aden, including searches of a large number of individual homes and the interrogation of many people.[204] AQAP attacks in areas where the Southern Movement is strong may therefore seek to increase anti-government alienation in the south, and some Southern Movement activists already maintain that raids against al-Qaeda are used as cover to arrest members of their own movement who have nothing to do with the AQAP terrorists.[205] Moreover, AQAP does not have to realign the Southern Movement in any dramatic way to meet a number of key goals. Rather, it only needs to gain a trickle of recruits from the south and a widespread acceptance of its active presence in the southern portion of the country.

The government may also have made matters worse by suspending around 800 southern members of the armed forces without pay in the summer of 2010.[206] The reasons for the suspension have never been clearly explained, but it is at least possible that those suspended were deemed unreliable because of their southern roots. Such individuals are trained in military fields and have reason to feel aggrieved and angry with the Yemeni government. If the trend of purging southerners from the military continues, such individuals could make an excellent talent pool for AQAP to target in future recruitment campaigns. At the present time, many southerners nevertheless remain concerned about the danger of al-Qaeda attracting the government's military attention, including bombing, to their region, so it is not clear whether al-Qaeda will make significant progress in the south.[207]

As with many clandestine organizations, it is often difficult to discern how many members of AQAP there are in Yemen. In December 2009, Yemeni Foreign Minister Abu Bakr al-Qirbi stated that there were probably around 200-300 al-Qaeda "operatives" in Yemen.[208] In May 2010, President Obama's assistant for homeland security echoed this assessment, stating that there were probably several hundred al-Qaeda members in Yemen.[209] These estimates include only full-time professional terrorists and not supporters or sympathizers who might be brought into the organization at a later time. These potential terrorist recruits probably number in the thousands or even the tens of thousands. The 200-300 number might also be dated since it is often difficult to track AQAP growth, which occurs in two ways. The most straightforward way is for additional Yemenis to choose to join AQAP for whatever reasons might be compelling to them, probably disillusionment and anger with the Yemeni government or with local tribal leaders allied with that government. The second way is for foreign radicals to leave their own country or previous foreign bases of operation and join up with al-Qaeda forces in Yemen. This occurred most dramatically with Saudi radicals, but there are also recurring claims that radicals from Pakistan and Afghanistan may be moving their operations to Yemen in response to problems they are facing in those countries with local security forces and U.S. drone attacks.[210]

The composition of AQAP may also be important in evaluating its capabilities and resilience. In early 2010, Yemen's National Security Agency director stated that around 90 percent of the al-Qaeda fighters in Yemen are Yemeni nationals, and only around 10 percent foreigners.[211] This appears to be an unlikely and lopsided estimate, implying that relatively few Saudi members of al-Qaeda were able to reach Yemen after their leadership advised them to do so. This estimate also suggests that only a limited number of radicals have arrived from Pakistan, although other statements by the security forces indicated that both Saudi and Pakistani radicals in Yemen are a problem.[212] This evaluation may therefore be based on spurious information, but, if sincere, it indicates that Yemenis view AQAP as primarily composed of domestic radicals. Certainly, foreign radicals, including Saudis, would have a difficult time surviving within Yemen without help from Yemeni supporters, especially tribal leaders who see financial advantages in sheltering the non-Yemeni members of AQAP. This tribal involvement would normally restrain al-Qaeda terrorists from selecting targets which, if attacked, could lead to serious government retaliation against a particular tribal region. Nevertheless, a number of problems in Yemen can be overcome with money.

While AQAP's interest in spectacular acts of terrorism constitutes a frightening threat, it would be a mistake to focus on these activities in ways that gloss over the organization's progress in challenging the government within Yemen itself. Whereas AQAP has often been viewed primarily as a terrorism organization, it may well be emerging as more than that now. In particular, AQAP is potentially rising as an insurgent group willing to wage guerrilla war and contest control of portions of the Yemeni hinterland with the Yemeni government. One of the most dramatic indications of AQAP's increased willingness to fight as an insurgent force can be seen during August 2010 combat operations in the southern Yemen town of Loder. At this time, AQAP established a strong presence in the town of 80,000 people to the point that the Yemeni army felt required to distribute pamphlets requiring the residents to leave the urban center prior to a forthcoming battle.[213] Evacuating a town of this size is seldom necessary to defeat a handful of terrorists. Conversely, such a measure might be required to defeat a serious guerrilla force which the Yemeni army seemed to be facing. In another problematic indicator, the AQAP forces initially remained to contest control of Loder rather than attempting to escape with the departing civilians. These actions indicated a strong level of commitment to their cause, as well as perhaps some degree of contempt for the uncertain quality of Yemeni military forces. Government forces ultimately won the battle in Loder, but only after serious resistance by the militants that included the use of at least one ambush with a rocket propelled grenade (RPG) that killed 11 soldiers.[214] The fighting lasted for several days, and at least some AQAP members escaped.[215] Heavy casualties were not reported on either side, perhaps indicating that al-Qaeda was only attempting to make a limited political statement rather than a bloody last stand.[216] Such a withdrawal was probably a wise operational move, since the Yemeni government would eventually use artillery, airpower, and perhaps tanks to break any stalemate involving ground forces.

The Loder battle does not appear to have been an aberration; in September 2010, Yemeni Army units were again engaged in urban combat against al-Qaeda forces.[217] This time, the fight occurred in the Yemeni village of Hawta, which has a population of around 20,000 people. At least 8,000 of these people (and possibly a great deal more) were able to flee the village during the fighting.[218] Many others were prevented from leaving by al-Qaeda so that their presence could help shield the terrorists from artillery and airpower strikes, while complicating the tactical operations of the Yemeni ground forces.[219] This encounter was reported to have involved Yemeni army tanks and armored vehicles moving against an uncertain number of al-Qaeda members.

A more persistent indication of AQAP's growing assertiveness is its willingness to ambush or attack squad, platoon, and perhaps larger sized units of the Yemeni army. On August 27, 2010, for example, al-Qaeda militants with RPGs and machine guns attacked a group of soldiers near Zinjibar, the capital of in Abyan province, while they were eating dinner and killed 12 of them.[220] Earlier the same day, one soldier was killed and three wounded while on patrol in the southern province of Lahij.[221] Police units are also regularly attacked.[222] In one September 2010 assault on the coastal town of Zinjibar, al-Qaeda attackers on motorbikes used hit-and-run tactics against two separate police targets, indicating careful planning and effective execution of a synchronized mission. In this strike, the terrorists attacked police stations with RPGs and automatic weapons, and then quickly fled the area.[223] Some of the gunmen were reported to have been killed, while others escaped. AQAP also issued a "death list" in September with the names of 55 military, judiciary, and police officials targeted for assassination.[224] Such lists are a common feature of some insurgencies and a warning to the named officials that they must leave their posts or face death. Adding to the uncertainty has been al-Qaeda's occasional ability to kill or kidnap very senior security officials throughout the country, suggesting that anyone they target may be vulnerable.[225]

There are also some positive signs within Yemen's still halting efforts to control terrorism. In summer

2010, some of Yemen's tribal leaders in the areas south and east of Sana'a seemed to be reevaluating their views on the costs and benefits of sheltering al-Qaeda suspects in their areas. The harboring of such fugitives led to Yemeni military raids into their territory, and threatened to disrupt any patronage networks providing funds from Sana'a or Riyadh. Thus, both a key source of tribal income and overall security within tribal areas were threatened. In response to this evolving situation, tribal leaders from the important Abida and al-Ashraf tribes pledged that they would "stop harboring people wanted by the security forces or who are accused of belonging to al-Qaeda."[226] These pledges are interesting and positive developments, although the extent to which they are to be honored remains uncertain.

U.S. INTERESTS AND POLICIES INVOLVING YEMEN

Osama bin Laden and the al-Qaeda leadership have often viewed Yemen as having considerable potential for serving as a safe haven, and also a country which they might eventually provoke the United States into attacking so that they could wage war against U.S. military forces, such as they have done in Iraq and Afghanistan. The al-Qaeda leadership at the highest level has therefore shown a strong interest in inflicting "bleeding wars" on the United States and seems to view Yemen as having considerable potential in this regard.[227] The Egyptian intervention in Yemen during the 1960s is considered instructive in this regard. Egypt has been reported as suffering up to 20,000 casualties in unproductive fighting in North Yemen from 1962 through 1967.[228] Perhaps with this precedent in mind, bin Laden and his senior lieutenants have continued to view Yemen as a potential theater of war with a variety of possibilities for crippling U.S. power in the region. In this regard, Yemen seems similar to Afghanistan in ways that are of interest to the al-Qaeda leadership. The populations of both countries have a strong tribal component, rugged terrain, and central governments of limited capacity. Yemen, of course, does not, like Afghanistan, have a neighboring country where al-Qaeda insurgents might easily take sanctuary. Additionally, bin Laden's ability to influence events in Yemen at the current time is quite limited. He cannot overrule the indigenous AQAP leadership, and he is almost certainly not informed of the operational plans of the al-Qaeda radicals he has helped to inspire. Al-Qaeda forces in Yemen consider themselves to be their own affiliated movement and not a subordinate organization with its headquarters outside of the country. These individuals seem primarily interested in waging war against the Saleh regime at this time, although they are also deeply opposed to the United States and may continue to support terrorist actions against U.S. targets both in general and in response to specific U.S. activities in Yemen and the Middle East.

While the United States has dangerous and committed enemies in Yemen, its allies are much more tentative. The Yemeni leadership chose to ally itself with the United States in the aftermath of the 9/11 strikes for a variety of reasons, including a fear that failure to do so could lead the United States to view Yemen as an enemy.[229] President Bush is reported to have disliked President Saleh shortly after first encountering him in a November 27, 2001 meeting, perceiving that the Yemeni president remained an irritating, uncooperative, and unreliable ally.[230] Specific U.S. complaints about Yemen centered on issues such as short, lenient sentences for terrorists, rapid release for some terrorism suspects that the United States considered to be especially dangerous, concealing information on Yemeni terrorist networks from the United States, and a potential openness to negotiations with al-Qaeda. Some U.S. policymakers have acidly referred to Yemeni security policy at various times as "catch and release" for dangerous radicals.[231] Many U.S. counterterrorism officials were especially concerned when the Yemeni president refused to extradite two suspects in the U.S.S. *Cole* bombing to the United States on the grounds that there was no extradition treaty in place between the two countries and that extradition was prohibited by the Yemeni Constitution.[232] This explanation sounded more like an excuse than a reason to many U.S. security professionals on a matter that was of considerable concern to the United States. Unfortunately, extradition seems to be yet another hot button issue, indeed being forbidden by the Yemeni Constitution.[233]

The government of Yemen has often irritated U.S. policymakers, but it also had its own reasons for limiting cooperation with Washington, including the ferocious anti-Americanism which can be ignited in that country. In some respects, the potential strength of anti-Americanism in Yemen is surprising. Yemen has no direct involvement in the Arab-Israeli conflict, and U.S. policies toward the Israelis and Palestinians have virtually no practical impact on Yemen. The Yemenis also maintain only limited links to Iraq, although the Yemeni population was deeply opposed to both the 1991 and 2003 U.S.-led wars against that country. Nevertheless, the Yemeni population remains particularly sensitive to the perception that the United States or any other foreign power is seeking to dominate their country. Many Yemenis have a great deal of pride in their heritage as citizens of a country which, at least in the case of northern Yemen, was never ruled by a Western power. Yemeni culture also encourages individuals to think in terms of affinities.[234] Western observers have often noted the intense loyalty of Yemeni strangers to each other when they are outside of their own country. This affinity exists at the tribal, national, and ethnic level. Arabs in dispute with the West, such as Saddam Hussein, often seem to get the pronounced benefit of the doubt in any confrontation.

Unfortunately, anti-American sentiment in Yemen can have a strong impact on official policy, and Saleh's various efforts to limit cooperation with the United States occurred in the context of a weak regime that did not wish to implement unpopular policies. Anti-Americanism in Yemen has also manifested itself in some volatile and unexpected ways. One incident may be particularly instructive of this problem. It has already been noted that a senior Bush administration official dropped hints that the November 3, 2002 deaths of six al-Qaeda militants was the result of a U.S. Predator drone attack.[235] This revelation was made to the great anger of the Yemeni government, reportedly undermining the cover story that both nations had agreed to put forward. Nevertheless, within the U.S. leadership, any decision to make this information public was probably not seen as a disclosure that would become a serious problem later. The U.S. administration was cooperating with the Yemeni government and was never accused of deploying this system without the government's permission (Saleh eventually admitted that it was deployed with his permission).[236] The Predator strike also seems like the lightest of light footprints. It served as a substitute for a troop presence on the ground, and the strike in question produced no collateral damage. Yemeni sovereignty was not compromised, and no innocent people were killed or even disturbed by this strike. Reasonable Western observers may have concluded that this operation would not appear particularly controversial in Yemen if it became publicly known. Yet, this was not the case.

President Saleh initially reacted with angry denials of the Western reports of the Predator attack. The Yemeni government continued to reject this version of events for a year or so, but eventually stated that the reports were true, and that Yemen had authorized the United States to undertake this operation.[237] The Yemeni president's admission came slowly and painfully in response to unyielding public criticism of both the attack and the cover-up. This political confrontation seemed like an especially intense, and by Western standards perhaps unreasonable, response to a single drone strike that was carefully managed so as to avoid innocent casualties, but there were also some special circumstances. While the Yemeni public has a deeply ingrained distrust of the United States at almost any time, the strike did not come at an ordinary time. In 2002 and early 2003, the public debate over Saleh's decision to authorize the U.S. Predator attack occurred just as Washington was preparing to invade Iraq. When the United States followed through on this decision, the Yemeni public became virulently hostile to any cooperation with the United States on security issues. Large and angry street protests broke out in Yemen in March 2003 in response to the U.S. invasion of Iraq. Demonstrators reported to be in the "tens of thousands" marched on the U.S. embassy and were stopped by Yemeni security forces, with at least four dead.[238] It remains an open question whether the Yemen public would have been more receptive to the strike if it had occurred within a less sensitive time frame. Whatever the case, the Yemeni political culture remains deeply hostile to the concept of U.S. drones being used for any purpose in Yemen even if it is with the permission of the Yemeni government.[239]

In the current somewhat calmer regional environment, President Saleh is willing to acknowledge openly some military cooperation with the United States so long as it involves joint activities that in no way imply U.S. domination within the relationship. The Yemeni government has publicly acknowledged that it receives military assistance from the United States. This aid has expanded from a modest $4.3 million in 2006 to $66.8 million in 2009. General David Petraeus, then serving as the U.S. Central Command Commander, travelled to Yemen on July 26, 2009, as part of an effort to assess ways in which the United States might support Yemeni counterterrorism efforts. In meetings with President Saleh and other top officials, General Petraeus confirmed that the Obama Administration planned significant increases in aid to support counterterrorism efforts then going forward in Yemen.[240] These increases were especially salient in the 2010 security assistance budget which authorized $155 million for Yemen, a dramatic increase over the previous year.[241] This funding is primarily aimed at improving the weapons, equipment, and training of the Yemeni forces. A sizable portion of the U.S. aid is being directed at bolstering elite counterterrorism units and aviation assets. The aviation assets include transport aircraft, four *Huey* helicopters, and a program to upgrade 10 Russian-made M-17 ("*Hip*") helicopters already in the inventory.[242] These systems will be used by the Yemeni military to transport special operations troops when they are needed to provide a rapid response to an unfolding crisis such as those involving AQAP. The counterterrorism troops are also being supplied with 50 new tactical Humvees, night vision goggles, and modern combat communications systems.[243] To further support Yemen, President Obama and a number of U.S. Government spokesmen have publicly announced increased intelligence support for that country.[244] This is a form of aid that the Yemenis seem comfortable acknowledging, and they have even publicly requested additional U.S. intelligence backing. The Yemeni Foreign Minister al-Qirbi stated that it was the "responsibility" of countries with strong intelligence capabilities to warn countries such as Yemen about terrorist activities.[245]

While the current military relationship with the United States has not always been well received by the Yemeni public, the regime remains able to manage opposition to such ties. In an apparent response to Saleh's efforts to defuse any potential backlash, Sheikh Zindani has not publicly opposed Sana'a's decision to accept U.S. training assistance and technological support. Rather, he has stated, "We accept any cooperation in the framework of respect and joint interests, and we reject military occupation of our country [U.S. bases]. And we don't accept the return of colonialism."[246] Zindani thereby made a distinction between receiving aid and training, and accepting a military presence involving U.S. combat troops being sent to Yemen to wage war against AQAP. Zindani's willingness to make such a distinction is clearly the result of Saleh's skills as a master politician, since it is a position he would probably never take without prompting. Zindani has been identified as a "specifically designated global terrorist" by the U.S. Treasury Department, which maintains that he had a long history of anti-American and pro-al-Qaeda activity.[247] Saleh insists that the United States is mistaken about the cleric's involvement with past terrorist activity, but is also loathe to confront him because of his strong following in Yemen. Other radical clerics have called for Yemen's religious leadership to go further than Zindani in opposing U.S. activities in Yemen. In an audiotaped message, an individual claiming to be the fugitive American-born cleric, Anwar al-Awlaki, exhorted Yemeni religious leaders to expand their objections to U.S activities and called for the killing of any American military or intelligence officials involved with the training of Yemeni security forces. The tape was made by a journalist in the course of what he claims was an interview with Awlaki inside of Yemen. It is widely believed to be authentic, although this has not been verified by official sources.[248]

In July 2010, President Obama again stressed U.S. solidarity with Yemen by praising that country's determination to fight terrorist groups in a White House press release issued following a telephone conversation between Presidents Obama and Saleh.[249] In an NBC interview, the President answered a question about the relationship with the Yemeni government regarding terrorism by stating, "They are cooperating."[250] This assessment is a reasonable description of the current situation in Yemen, and for reasons already noted, President Saleh may be significantly more willing to cooperate with the United States than he was a few years earlier. Moreover, Saleh has now become so deeply involved in the conflict with AQAP that he cannot easily back away from it and treat al-Qaeda as though it were just another Yemeni political faction. The Yemeni president also knows that he needs resources to pursue enemies that are much tougher and more radical than they were a decade ago. Saleh therefore continues to weigh carefully what he can do and must avoid within the context of Yemeni political culture. President Obama, for his part, has continued to support Saleh beyond the issue of terrorism and emphasized U.S. support for a unified Yemen.[251]

One remaining problem that is probably more significant for Washington than Sana'a involves the Guantanamo Bay, Cuba, detainees. In mid-2010, the United States held over 100 Yemenis in custody at Guantanamo Bay for terrorism-related offenses with the final disposition of these prisoners remaining uncertain. President Obama has indicated that he does not wish them to be returned to Yemen under current circumstances for incarceration there. One of the reasons for this decision involves the ongoing security problems in Yemeni prisons and other detention facilities which manifested themselves in the 2006 jailbreak. In this case, the guards may have been untrustworthy. A different set of problems was seen in June 2010 when al-Qaeda fighters stormed a security facility in Aden, leading to the release of several prisoners.[252] Adding to these problems, the Yemeni de-radicalization programs have largely been failures, especially when compared with the much more successful Saudi programs. Riyadh's de-radicalization efforts are extremely well-funded and make strong use of Saudi tribal and family responsibilities to prevent released prisoners from recidivism. Former terrorists are also sometimes provided with a stipend to give them an additional incentive to stay out of trouble. The now-defunct Yemeni program, by contrast, was largely a program centered on detainees receiving religious guidance from one Islamic judge who, while respected, did not seem to change many minds. Likewise, the radicals enrolled in this program were expected to sign pledges to support the Yemeni government. These pledges had little, if any, value in the absence of a more comprehensive agenda. Recognizing that this program was not effective, Yemeni authorities discontinued it in 2005.[253] The Yemeni government seldom seems particularly concerned about getting its detainees back and may be satisfied to allow them to remain in U.S. prisons.

CONCLUSION AND RECOMMENDATIONS

The problems in Yemen defy easy answers and are often viewed as so overwhelming that they can be approached only in a tentative, trial-and-error manner. The United States must therefore remain aware of the potential for the situation to get worse in Yemen before it gets better. Moreover, Yemen's security difficulties are so interrelated that it is difficult to solve the al-Qaeda problem in any fundamental way without some progress in managing the other difficulties in Yemen. President Obama's statement that he has "no intention" of sending troops to Yemen is reassuring to most Yemenis and indicates reasonable concern over the danger of falling into a significant military intervention. Such an intervention would consume U.S. lives and resources and could only make the security situation in the region increasingly unstable. This set of problems does not require the United States to remain aloof from Yemen's problems. Rather, it suggests that Washington's involvement in Yemen must be structured in ways that the political culture will accept. Unfortunately, for the time being the United States may have to focus on helping Yemen contain or manage problems rather than solve them.

The difficulties associated with managing Yemen policy should nevertheless not be allowed to obfuscate the high stakes of the current situation in Yemen. There are important reasons for defeating al-Qaeda in Yemen, even if this does not destroy the organization and instead leads it to move operations to more hospitable sanctuaries in remote parts of the world. Yemen is central in the struggle against al-Qaeda due to its key strategic location, including a 700-mile border with Saudi Arabia. It also dominates one of the region's key waterways, the Bab al-Mandeb strait, which controls access to the southern Red Sea. Furthermore, the problem of Yemen-based terrorism remains an important international threat which cannot be ignored. The U.S. leadership may have narrowly escaped unmanageable domestic pressure for an additional war in the Middle East when the Christmas bomber plot was thwarted in late 2009. If this incompetent enemy had actually been able to detonate his explosives, the call for a hard-line military response would have been difficult to resist. Yet, an actual invasion of Yemen would have produced a vicious indigenous response that would have been difficult to contain. Moreover, any effort to rebuild, modernize, and democratize Yemen in the aftermath of such an intervention would make the problems of Afghanistan and Iraq look simple by comparison. While paying special attention to Yemeni sensitivities about foreign influence, the United States must do what it can to prevent Yemen from falling into a cauldron of radicalism *before* the subject of intervention even arises.

The Yemeni political system is likely to remain unstable, and the economic system is likely to remain impoverished, for the foreseeable future. Central governmental authority in the hinterland can be expected to remain limited for the foreseeable future. It is also possible that the country could collapse into anarchy over the next decade or so as the current problems continue to intensify. Helping Yemen manage these problems will be difficult since a constant distrust of U.S. actions is always present in Yemeni politics. Within this especially difficult milieu, this report makes the following recommendations.

1. **The United States must not seek to Americanize the conflicts in Yemen, and should avoid sending major combat units there. However bad the situation may become in Yemen, Americanizing the war against AQAP can only make it dramatically worse.** Yemeni public opposition to the presence of ground troops with combat missions is almost universal, and it is possible that large elements of the Yemeni public would rise against their president and parliament if the government invited the United States to provide such forces. Certainly, the Yemeni clergy is particularly shrill on this subject, and this intensity goes far beyond the strident voices of well-known radicals such as Sheikh Zindani. The United States should understand that an alliance with Yemen can only go so far, and that the Yemeni government has good reasons for limiting its public cooperation with the United States.

2. **The United States needs to continue supplying intelligence, training, and military equipment to Yemen so long as these assets directly support counterterrorism missions.** So far, the United States has been highly effective in tailoring its military aid to Yemen in ways that focus on the needs of the counter-al-Qaeda mission. Small units of elite troops with a rapid movement capability can be extremely effective in dealing

with terrorists, although their ability to add capabilities to deal with problems in the Houthi areas or the activities of the Southern Movement are much more limited. Should AQAP be able to develop into a widespread and effective insurgent force, the United States will have to expand aid in ways that are less counterterrorism focused. The United States will then have do everything possible to avoid becoming viewed as a party to Yemen's other conflicts. The United States must also structure its military support to Yemen in ways that continue to enhance a long-term military relationship between the two countries and expose the Yemenis to U.S. concepts of military professionalism. Such an approach would include particular vigilance in providing ongoing opportunities for Yemeni officers to train in the United States in programs such as the Professional Military Education (PME) courses. Such courses give international officers an opportunity to forge close relationships with American officers and to consider the importance of respect for human rights within a military context. To the extent possible, U.S. military training programs and educational opportunities must also share relevant counterinsurgency doctrine and expertise with the Yemeni military, and help them rise above an "Operation Scorched Earth" mentality.

3. **The United States, and particularly the U.S. military assistance program for Yemen, needs to recognize and respond to the changing nature of the al-Qaeda threat in Yemen.** AQAP is no longer simply a terrorist group, although that organization's potential to do harm through spectacular acts of terrorism remains undiminished. It is now an insurgent organization capable of waging sustained combat against government forces. It is also apparently capable of es-

tablishing itself in those territories where the government traditionally exercises little authority so long as AQAP can co-opt or intimidate the local tribal leadership in these areas. This danger suggests that the United States may have to expand its military assistance to Yemen, while maintaining as light a footprint as possible and avoiding the deployment of U.S. troops for anything other than training. Military planners need to consider ways to address the problems that may be associated with an expanded aid program, while seeking continued input from those on the ground on how such programs can be improved.

4. **U.S. leadership must remain aware of the severe limitations of the Yemeni government in controlling its own territory, but it must also understand that there are no serious alternatives to the Saleh regime in dealing with the current threats to the region and the world emanating from Yemen.** The United States must also maintain an ongoing and comprehensive dialogue with the Yemenis on ways that al-Qaeda can be defeated in Yemen. It might also be considered that President Obama is more popular in the Arab World than most previous American presidents due to his well-received outreach efforts to the Muslim world. It may be possible that Yemen will find cooperation with President Obama to be less domestically controversial than cooperation with his predecessors.

5. **The United States should continue to push for peaceful solutions of the Sa'ada difficulties and the Yemeni government's problems with the Southern Movement.** The United States should not abandon its support for a one-Yemen policy without strong and ongoing provocation from the Yemeni government. If it eventually does consider revising this policy, it should do so only after careful discussions and coor-

dination with regional allies. This is not because the southern Yemeni cause is without merit, but rather because any U.S. intervention in sensitive internal issues can sometimes create new problems for all involved parties. The danger of the south fragmenting into a series of competing mini-states also needs to be considered, as such a development could harm regional security and provide al-Qaeda with increased opportunities for alliances and sanctuary. The key problem for the United States in leaving the issues of the Southern Movement unaddressed is that the current frustration of the southerners may lead to increased radicalization over time. Al-Qaeda is clearly trying to harness the energy of the Southern Movement for its own ends. While most southerners seem repelled by al-Qaeda, this may not continue for the indefinite future if frustration levels are allowed to rise. It is therefore imperative that the Yemeni government dramatically improve its governance activities in the south and avoid policies that cause southerners to feel exploited by the government.

6. **The expansion of good governance in Yemen is important, and any U.S. efforts to support this goal need to be carefully considered in consultation with Yemeni leaders.** The Yemeni population has a number of needs that must be addressed in the short term before democratic expansion becomes discussable. There is deeply entrenched corruption in Yemen that is part of the political culture. The United States has not been able to halt the rampant corruption in Afghanistan, Iraq, and Pakistan, and it cannot be expected to implement fundamental ameliorative changes in Yemen. Nevertheless, ways need to be found to reduce corruption to the point that the intentions of important international aid projects are not subverted.

7. **The United States should support the work of effective and trustworthy nongovernmental organizations (NGOs) in Yemen.** The United States cannot solve the problem of al-Qaeda in Yemen with development aid administered by U.S. personnel, but it can certainly encourage and support the work of responsible NGOs, and ask other developed countries to do the same. Their role is vital since there are relatively few individuals in the Yemeni government who can impartially administer well-funded development programs. Such programs will have to address a myriad of economic problems in order to help Yemen in a meaningful way. Programs to help address the severe and rising problem of unemployment, particularly among young people, may be especially important. The Yemeni bureaucracy is not up to many of the tasks associated with development since it is both riddled with internal problems and maintains only a limited ability to operate outside of Sana'a. This situation greatly magnifies the importance of NGOs.

8. **The United States needs to involve Saudi Arabia in efforts to help Yemen, while recognizing that U.S. and Saudi interests in Yemen will not always coincide.** So long as it remains Yemen's largest aid donor, Saudi Arabia will always have a great deal to say about Yemen's future actions. The Saudis also have tremendous concern about al-Qaeda activities in Yemen, having endured a terrorist bombing campaign within their own country which reached its height around 2004-05. Also, as noted, al-Qaeda forces in Yemen remain interested in striking at Saudi targets to the extent they are able to do so as indicated by the nearly successful effort to murder Prince Mohammad bin Nayef. Nevertheless, Saudi Arabia can be seen to play a negative role to the extent that it funds and encourages clerics and Islamic organizations that en-

gage in activities which harm Zaydi-Shafei relations. The United States therefore needs to encourage Saudi Arabia to follow policies that indicate respect for, or at least a limited tolerance of, Zaydi Islam. While the Saudis may not truly feel such respect, they have a vested interest in preventing the Houthis from turning to Iran as their only regional sympathizer and ally. Since current tensions between Riyadh and Tehran are quite high, this is a concern worth repeating and emphasizing in dialogue with the Saudis.

9. **The United States may also want to consider encouraging other Arab allies beyond Saudi Arabia to take a more active role in helping Yemen, although such plans will have to be discussed with both Sana'a and Riyadh in considerable detail.** It is, for example, possible that the Jordanian government could serve as an increasingly useful ally in supporting Yemen. The Amman leadership detests al-Qaeda and has a long history of cooperating with Gulf Arab states in working against the organization. This cooperation includes counterterrorism training at the King Abdullah II Special Operations Training Center (KASOTC). Additionally, if Iraq is able to bring its own problems under control to the point that it can direct serious attention to regional problems, it may wish to resume military-to-military cooperation with Yemen in ways that encourage the Yemenis to avoid total dependency on Riyadh. It is also possible that Yemeni military forces could benefit from increased combined exercises with other Arab states and even peacekeeping training. Again, the role of Jordan could be useful in teaching Yemen troops how to address some security problems with minimum force being directed at the population in conflict areas. While the Jordanian approach to this issue specializes in interna-

tional peacekeeping, some of the principles used in an international environment may be relevant to places such as Sa'ada province and various trouble spots in southern Yemen. Jordan maintains a Peacekeeping Operations Center Based in Zarqa. Since 1989, 61,000 Jordanian troops have participated in peacekeeping operations in 18 conflict areas, giving them a wealth of information and experience that Yemen may find useful.[254] Since Jordan is not a wealthy country, funding from the United States, European Union, wealthy Arab states, or elsewhere would be needed to move forward on such efforts.

10. **The United States must remain aware of potential Iranian activities in Yemen, while bearing in mind that Yemeni charges of Iranian intervention in the Houthi rebellion remain unproven and difficult to evaluate.** If the Yemenis have presented any proof to the United States of Iranian involvement in northern Yemen, they have not done so publicly. Moreover any secret proof made available to Washington has remained secret in a way that is unusual in Washington. However, we do not know that Iran is involved. Tehran could certainly be playing a role in Yemen, while leaving only the lightest of footprints. In particular, Yemeni rebels do not require weapons transfers from outsiders like Iran in order to wage war against the government. Weapons are so widely available in Yemen that this is probably one of the least effective strategies for supporting the rebels. Rather, Houthi insurgents need money to keep their cause alive, and transfers of funds are more difficult to ascertain or prove.

11. **The United States must not assume that Saudi de-radicalization programs will work well with Yemeni radicals.** It must also accept the fact that the Ye-

meni de-radicalization programs have turned out to be failures for reasons related to both funding and national culture. The Saudi system has mostly succeeded because the former radicals are carefully reintegrated into society, with good jobs and encouragement to marry if they have not already done so. The former radicals are placed under the close supervision of senior members of their families and tribes who will be held responsible if they return to jihadi activity. This skillful blend of carrots and sticks means that ex-radicals would have to give up a comfortable life style and betray their family in order to return to jihadi activities. While some of them do so, many do not. Yemen is totally unable to recreate this system, and placing Yemeni jihadis in the Saudi program will not lead to successful results since the Yemenis will move beyond the reach of Saudi security forces and the Saudi incentive structure for remaining out of trouble once they return to Yemen.

12. **U.S. officials, including military officials, must resist all temptations to take public credit for and celebrate military victories that might occur against al-Qaeda forces in Yemen.** While U.S. support for Yemen is important and must be continued and accelerated, both the U.S. administration and the U.S. Government agencies involved in fighting terrorism must not contribute to the misperception that Washington is running the war. U.S. officials who openly congratulate themselves about U.S. victories are hurting the cause they profess to help. Praising the Yemeni government for these victories will have to be sufficient.

13. **As in Iraq and Afghanistan, the United States will have to be tolerant of the Yemeni government's willingness to pardon and rehabilitate former mem-**

bers of al-Qaeda that have not been involved in international terrorism and show good prospects for remaining outside of terrorist groups in the future. If the Yemeni government wishes to pardon them for attacks on the Yemeni military, that is an internal affair so long as measures are taken to ensure that repentant terrorists never rejoin al-Qaeda or similar groups. What the Yemenis must not do is pardon terrorists and then fail to keep track of them or their activities. Foreign assistance in the use of bio-metric data might be an option worth considering in these instances.

ENDNOTES

1. For a complete video of President Obama's speech, see "Obama Promises Justice for Christmas Terror Plotters," *CNN.com*, January 2, 2010.

2. U.S. Congress, Senate Committee on Armed Services, *U.S. Policy on Afghanistan, Pakistan*, Statement of David H. Petraeus Commander U.S. Central Command, 111th Cong., April 1, 2009.

3. As cited in Murad Batal al-Shishani, "Yemeni Clerics Announce Mandatory Jihad Against Foreign Intervention," *Jamestown Foundation Terrorism Monitor*, Vol. 8, No. 4, January 28, 2010.

4. Saudi Arabia, at around 28 million people, technically has a larger population, although over 5 million of these people are non-nationals (including Yemenis) who have come to the country to work. If one subtracts non-nationals from the Saudi total, then the two countries have an almost equal number of people at the present time.

5. Jeffrey D. Feltman, Assistant Secretary, Bureau of Near Eastern Affairs, U.S. Department of State, and Robert F. Godec, Principal Deputy Coordinator for Counterterrorism, U.S. Department of State, "Yemen on the Brink: Implications of U.S. Policy: Statement before the House Committee on Foreign Affairs," State Department Press Release, February 3, 2010. Testimony on popu-

lation included in this study is based on an U.S. Agency for International Development (USAID) funded study. Other sources have lower projections.

6. At that time, Arab politicians applied the word "republic" to virtually all post-monarchical systems of government regardless of whether they held elections or not.

7. An imamate is a form of Islamic government which in Yemen combined temporal and religious leadership in a single individual of distinguished heritage.

8. Paul Dresh, *A History of Modern Yemen*, New York: Cambridge University Press, 2000, pp. 89-90.

9. One scholar chose to describe the imam as "prehistoric." See Malcolm Kerr, *The Arab Cold War*, New York: Oxford University Press, 1970, p. 26.

10. The author has discussed the evolution of this war in W. Andrew Terrill, "The Chemical Warfare Legacy of the Yemen War," *Comparative Strategy*, Vol. 10, No. 2, 1991, pp. 109-119. Also see Ali Abdel Rahman Rahmy, *The Egyptian Policy in the Arab World: Intervention in Yemen 1962-1967*, Washington, DC: University Press of America, Inc., 1983.

11. Terrill, "The Chemical Warfare Legacy of the Yemen War." The Egyptian military had not integrated chemical weapons (CW) into its order of battle well, nor did it seem to have developed detailed doctrine for CW use, although they did become more effective over time.

12. President Nasser promised to remove all troops from Yemen at the September 1967 Khartoum Arab Summit Conference as a condition of receiving Saudi aid. In a February 1968 meeting with President Aref of Iraq, he stated that all Egyptian troops had been withdrawn from Yemen. See "Document: The Meeting between Nasser and Abdel Rahman Aref, 10 February 1968," as cited in Abdel Majid Farid, *Nasser the Final Years*, Reading, United Kingdom (UK): Ithaca Press, 1994, p. 115.

13. Anthony Nutting, *Nasser*, New York: E. P. Dutton & Company, 1972, p. 338; Said K. Aburish, *Nasser: The Last Arab*, New York: St. Martin's Press, 2004, p. 228.

14. Robert D Burrowes, "The Famous Forty and Their Companions: North Yemen's First-generation Modernists and Educational Emigrants," *The Middle East Journal*, Vol. 59, No. 1, Winter 2005, pp. 81-97.

15. Aden became a Crown Colony in 1937. Outside of Aden, the protectorate relationship was set up through a large number of agreements with local southern tribal leaders.

16. The GPC won 123 seats, Islah won 62, and the YAR won 56. Notable irregularities occurred in the election. See Dresch, p. 194.

17. In the 2003 parliamentary elections, the YAR obtained a pathetic 8 seats in the 301-person parliament.

18. Victoria Clark, *Yemen: Dancing on the Heads of Snakes*, New Haven, CT: Yale University Press, 2010, p. 108.

19. Kevin Peraino and Michael Hirsh, "Our Man in Yemen," *Newsweek*, January 18, 2010, p. 36.

20. See April Longley Alley, "The Rules of the Game: Unpacking Patronage Politics in Yemen," *Middle East Journal*, Vol. 64, No 3, Summer 2010, pp. 385-409.

21. *Ibid.;* also see Clark, p. 191.

22. Ed Blanche, "Saudis lead the charge against al-Qaeda," *The Middle East*, February 2010, p. 15; and Steven Erlanger, "In Yemen, U.S. Faces Leader Who Puts Family First," *New York Times*, January 5, 2010.

23. Clark, p. 227.

24. *Ibid.*, p. 159.

25. Steven Erlanger, "At Yemen College, Scholarship and Jihadist Ideas," *New York Times*, January 19, 2010.

26. Most scholarly literature lists Saleh's year of birth as 1942. The president's website lists it as 1946, but this may be a mistake or an attempt to claim that he is younger than is actually the case. The same website claims Saleh joined the armed forces in 1958 which would make him a child soldier of 12 if he was born in 1946. Information available from *presidentsaleh.gov.ye*.

27. Direct Presidential elections took place in Yemen for the first time in 1999 and then again in 2006. As noted, parliamentary elections had already occurred earlier.

28. Two important examples of this possibility occurred with bloodless coups in Qatar in 1995 and Oman in 1970. On Qatar, see Mary Ann Tetreault, "Gulf Winds: Inclement Political Weather in the Arabian Peninsula, *Current History*, January 1996, pp. 24-25. On the British supported coup in Oman, see Calvin Allen, Jr., and W. Lynn Rigsbee II, *Oman Under Qaboos: From Coup to Constitution, 1970-1996*, London, UK: Frank Cass, 2000, p. 28-29.

29. "Weapons Galore in Yemen," *Yemen Times*, April 22, 2010.

30. Christopher Boucek, *Yemen: Avoiding a Downward Spiral,"* Carnegie Paper No. 109, Washington, DC: Carnegie Endowment for International Peace, September 2009, pp. 6-8.

31. "Al-Qaeda Benefits from Yemen woes—PM," *Jordan Times*, January 29, 2010.

32. "Hunger in Yemen could spark unrest, exodus—UN," *Jordan Times*, May 5, 2010.

33. Dresh, p. 208.

34. "Yemen," *CIA World Factbook 2010,"* available from *www.cia.gov*.

35. "Yemen Tightens Security," *Kuwait Times*, March 18, 2010.

36. Sarah Phillips, *What Comes Next in Yemen? Al-Qaeda, the Tribes, and State-Building*, Washington, DC: Carnegie Endowment

for International Peace, Middle East Program, No. 107, March 2010, p. 2.

37. Yemeni officials consistently deny the nature of the crisis, suggesting that new oil explorations and improved security for pipelines and oil infrastructure will extend the significance of the Yemeni oil industry for some time to come. There is no real evidence for this view. See "Yemen maintains vibrant oil sector," United Press International, August 20, 2010.

38. Christopher Boucek, *Yemen: Avoiding a Downward Spiral,"* Carnegie Paper No. 109, Washington, DC: Carnegie Endowment for International Peace, September 2009, p. 5.

39. "Yemen LNG exports first shipment of natural gas to South Korea," *Yemen Observer*, November 5, 2009.

40. Mohamed Sudam, "Yemen Gunmen Kill 2 Belgian Tourists and 2 Yemenis," *Reuters*, January 18, 2008.

41. Ahmad al-Haj, "Yemen upholds death sentences in U.S. Embassy attack," *Washington Times*, July 11, 2010.

42. Daniel Martin Varisco, "On the Meaning of Chewing: The Significance of Qat (*catha edulis*) in the Yemen Arab Republic," *International Journal of Middle East Studies*, Vol. 18, No. 1, 1986, p. 1.

43. *Ibid.*

44. Qat draws water, life from Yemen," *Kuwait Times*, May 29, 2009.

45. See Robert D. Burrowes and Catherine M. Kasper, "The Salih Regime and the Need for a Credible Opposition," *Middle East Journal*, Vol. 61, No. 2, Spring 2007, p. 264. Others cited in this article have suggested that this characterization is unduly harsh.

46. *Ibid.*, pp. 265-266.

47. Transparency International, Corruption Perceptions Index (CPI) 2009, available from *www.transparency.org*.

48. Burrowes and Kasper, p. 265, n. 10.

49. Joseph Kostiner, "Yemen," in *Middle East Contemporary Survey 2000*, Vol. XXIV, Bruce Maddy-Weitzman, ed., Tel Aviv, Israel: Tel Aviv University, 2002, p. 630.

50. Ahmed al-Haj, "Yemen says al-Qaida is government's main challenge," *Associated Press*, August 29, 2010.

51. "Multiple Conflicts Strain Yemen's ability to strike against al-Qaeda," *Gulf in the Media, Associated Press*, January 10, 2010, available from *corp.gulfinthemedia.com*.

52. Gregory D. Johnsen, " The Expansion Strategy of Al Qa'ida in the Arabian Peninsula, *West Point Combating Terrorism Center Sentinel*, January 2010, p. 6.

53. Mohammad bin Sallam, "Explosions in the South," *Yemen Times*, September 16, 2010.

54. See Hassan al-Haifi, "Common Sense: When is Killing Civilians Legitimate or Illegitimate? The Innocent Always Pay the Heaviest Price," *Yemen Times*, June 6, 2010.

55. Clark, p. 248.

56. "Saudis held briefly by Yemeni rebels," *Arab News*, April 25, 2010.

57. Mohamed Ghobari and Raissa Kasolowsky, "Yemen's al-Qaeda calls for jihad, fighting in north," *Reuters*, February 8, 2010.

58. "Saudi Air Force hits Yemen rebels after border raid," *Jordan Times*, November 6, 2009.

59. Robert F. Worth, "Yemen Seems to Reject Cease-Fire with Rebels," *New York Times*, February 1, 2010.

60. "No Changes in border with Yemen, says Prince Khaled," *Arab News*, March 7, 2010.

61. "Yemen war with Shi'ite rebels is over: president," *Khaleej Times Online*, March 19, 2010.

62. Hammoud Mounassar, "At least 49 killed in north Yemen clashes: Rebels," AFP, July 21, 2010.

63. "At least 40 killed in north Yemen Clashes," AFP, July 21, 2010.

64. "GCC Chief Hails Outcome of Yemen Talks in Doha," *Gulf Times*, August 31, 2010.

65. "Yemeni officials, rebels reach deal in Qatar," *Daily Star*, Beirut, August 28, 2010,

66. Saleh is a "non-Hashemite" Zaydi and therefore, unlike Hashemite Zaydis, not considered to be descended from Islam's Prophet, Mohammad. See Barak A. Salmoni, Bryce Loidolt, and Madeleine Wells, *Regime and Periphery in Northern Yemen: The Huthi Phenomenon*, Santa Monica, CA: Rand National Defense Research Institute, 2010, p. 23.

67. Clark, p. 40.

68. "Yemen's War: Pity Those Caught in the Middle," *Economist*, November 21, 2009, p. 49.

69. *Yemen: Defusing the Saada Time Bomb*, Brussels, Belgium: International Crisis Group (ICG), May 27, 2009, p. 12.

70. *Ibid.*, p. 10.

71. Saddam al-Ashmori, "Yemen Weapons Dealer Released," *Yemen Times*, June 21, 2010.

72. See A. Salmoni, Loidolt, and Wells, p. 2.

73. "Yemeni army aims to 'save' civilians," *The Peninsula*, August 16, 2009.

74. "Yemen's Elusive Peace Deal: A Bloody Blame Game," *Economist*, February 6, 2010, p. 52.

75. Stephen Day, *The Political Challenge of Yemen's Southern Movement,* Washington, DC: Carnegie Endowment for International Peace, Middle East Program, No. 108, March 2010, p. 4.

76. Clark, p. 255.

77. Sheila Carapico, "Yemen and the Aden-Abyan Islamic Army," *Middle East Report* (MERIP) *Online,* October 18, 2000.

78. Joseph Kostiner, "Yemen," *Middle East Contemporary Survey,* Vol. XVIII: 1994, Ami Ayalon, Bruce Maddy-Weitzman, eds., Boulder, CO: Westview Press, 1996, p. 709.

79. Dresch, p. 194.

80. Clark, p. 144.

81. Some of the officers' grievances were belatedly addressed in a gracious manner in the apparent hope that such generosity would help to undermine the Southern Movement. This strategy was implemented too late to make much difference in slowing the movement's popularity. See Stephen Day, "Updating Yemeni National Unity: Could Lingering Regional Divisions Bring Down the Regime?" *Middle East Journal,* Vol. 62, No. 3, Summer 2008, p. 428.

82. *Ibid.,* p. 418.

83. "Five Killed at South Yemen Rally," BBC News, November 25, 2009, available from *news .bbc.co.uk.*

84. Nicole Stracke and Mohammed Saif Haidar, *The Southern Movement in Yemen,* Dubai, United Arab Emirates (UAE): Gulf Research Center and Sheba Center for Strategic Studies, April 2010, pp. 2-3.

85. "Thousands Rally Across South Yemen for Independence," *Kuwait Times,* February 28, 2010.

86. "Yemeni forces deployed in Aden to control separatists," *Kuwait Times,* December 1, 2009.

87. Agence France Presse, AFP, "Yemen court jails southern activists for 'harming unity'," *Daily Star*, March 31, 2010.

88. "Opposition allied with armed foes of the state: Yemen," *The Peninsula*, April 26, 2010.

89. "Prison Sentences for Southern Movement Activists," *Yemen Times*, January 4, 2010.

90. Mohammad Bin Sallam, "Protests in the Southern Governorates," *Yemen Times*, July 12, 2010.

91. *In the Name of Unity: The Yemeni Government's Brutal Response to Southern Movement Protests*, New York: Human Rights Watch, December 2009, pp. 6, 25-28.

92. Salmoni, Loidolt, and Wells, p. 37.

93. Stracke and Haidar, pp. 3-4.

94. Ahmed al-Haj, "Gunmen attack government convoy in south Yemen," *Arab News*, May 15, 2010.

95. Stracke and Haidar, pp. 5-6.

96. Clark, p. 149.

97. "Civil War Fears as Yemen Celebrates Unity," BBC News, May 21, 2009.

98. Ginny Hill, "What is Happening in Yemen?" *Survival*, Vol. 52, No. 2, April-May 2010, p. 110.

99. *The Political Challenge of Yemen's Southern Movement*, p. 9.

100. Zaid al-Alaya'a, "Al-Qaeda Announces support of southern movement in Yemen," *Yemen Observer*, May 16, 2009.

101. Clark, p. 245; "Criticism of Yemeni offensive mounts," United Press International, August 27, 2010.

102. Nadia al-Sakkkaf, "Al-Qaeda Steps Up its Tactics as the Government Strikes Harder," *Yemen Times*, September 16, 2010.

103. "Yemen war with Shi'ite rebels is over: president," *Khaleej Times Online*, March 19, 2010.

104. "Opposition allied with armed foes of the state: Yemen," *The Peninsula*, April 26, 2010.

105. "Policemen killed in south Yemen in clashes with rebels," *BBC News*, March 1, 2010.

106. Salmoni, Loidolt, and Wells, p. 36.

107. See "Yemen Leader's Rule Presents Thorny Issues for US," *New York Times*, January 5, 2010; *Jane's Sentinal Country Risk Assessments, Yemen, External Affairs*, Jane's Information Group, January 8, 2010.

108. Dresch, p. 185; James A. Baker III, *The Politics of Diplomacy: Revolution, War and Peace, 1989-1992*, New York: G. P. Putnam's Sons, 1995, p. 317.

109. Clark, p. 170.

110. Dresch, p. 185.

111. Lawrence Freedman and Efraim Karsh, *The Gulf Conflict, 1900-1991, Diplomacy and War in the New World Order*, Princeton, NJ: Princeton University Press, 1993, pp. 231-232.

112. Dresch, p. 186.

113. Varisco, p. 2.

114. Clark, p. 140.

115. Eric Watkins, "Promise Them Anything," *The Middle East*, September 1994, p. 8.

116. Kostiner, *MECS*, Vol. XVIII, p. 704.

117. John Duke Anthony, "Saudi Arabian-Yemeni Relations: Implications for U.S. Policy," *Middle East Policy*, Vol. VII, No. 3, June 2000, p. 83.

118. Alfred Hermida, "Civil War Breaks Out in Yemen," *Middle East International*, May 13, 1994, p. 4.

119. Anthony, p. 92.

120. *Ibid.*, p. 85.

121. "Saudi Company Establishes Training Center for Yemeni Workers," *Yemen Observer*, January 6, 2009.

122. Ulf Laessing, "Saudi-Western Interests in Yemen not identical," *Kuwait Times*, January 26, 2010.

123. King Fahd had been incapacitated with a stroke since November 1995, and Abdullah was therefore the *de facto* ruler of the kingdom.

124. Askar H. al-Enazy, *The Long Road from Taaif to Jeddah: Resolution of a Saudi Yemeni Boundary Dispute*, Abu Dhabi, UAE: The Emirates Center for Strategic Studies and Research, 2005, pp. 43-50.

125. Brian Whitaker, "Tensions with the Saudis," *Middle East International*, December 19, 1997.

126. Representative Adam B. Schiff, "The Challenge of Yemen," *Yemen Times*, April 24, 2010.

127. Agence France-Presse. "HRW urges Yemen donors to link aid to human rights." *Daily Star*, March 29, 2010.

128. Clark, p. 219.

129. Ginny Hill, "Yemen: Fear of Failure: *Chatham House: Briefing Paper*, November 2008, p. 5.

130. For a useful overview of differences between these two countries, see Frederic Wehrey *et al.*, *Saudi-Iranian Relations Since*

the Fall of Saddam, Santa Monica, CA: RAND Corporation, 2009; also see Richard Javad Heydarian, "Iran-Saudi Rivalry Deepens," *Asia Times*, August 11, 2010; Paul Handley, "Huge Saudi Arms Deal Aimed at Iran, Yemen," *Kuwait Times*, September 16, 2010.

131. Ted Galen Carpenter and Malou Innocent, "The Iraq War and Iranian Power," *Survival*, Winter 2007-08, pp. 67-82.

132. See, for example, "Iran Spies in Yemeni Court," *Kuwait Times*, April 13, 2010; Sudarsan Raghavan, "Yemen's Fight with Rebels a Regional Concern: Sunni-Shiite Tensions Grow as Saudis Allege Iran's Involvement," *Washington Post*, November 14, 2009.

133. Robert Lacey, *Inside the Kingdom: Kings, Clerics, Modernists, Terrorists, and the Struggle for Saudi Arabia*, New York: Viking, 2009, p. 245.

134. Blanche, "Saudis lead the charge against al-Qaeda," p. 15.

135. Caryle Murphy, "AQAP's Growing Security Threat to Saudi Arabia," *West Point Combating Terrorism Center Sentinel*, June 2010, p. 1.

136. Some sources have expressed doubt about Wahayshi's ability to lead the organization which they characterize as highly factionalized. See Nicole Stracke, "Al-Qaeda in Yemen—Still a Manageable Threat," *Gulf Research Center Analysis*, June 23, 2009.

137. Robert F. Worth, "Freed by U.S., Saudi Becomes a Qaeda Chief," *New York Times*, January 23, 2009.

138. As cited in Sarah Phillips, p. 3.

139. Blanche, "Saudis lead the charge against al-Qaeda," p. 14.

140. Osama bin Laden's Saudi citizenship was revoked in 1994.

141. "'Bin Laden's bodyguard' in Court," *BBC News* January 12, 2006; Tim Butcher, "My Life in Al-Qa'eda, by bin Laden's bodyguard," March 27, 2008, available from *Telegraph.co.uk*.

142. Steve Coll, *The Bin Ladens: An Arabian Family in the American Century*, New York: Penguin Books, 2008, p. 564. Note that child marriages in the rural areas of Yemen often involve brides between 12 and 14 years old, with some as young as 10. On child brides in Yemen, see "Top Yemeni Clerics Oppose Ban on Child Brides," *Jordan Times*, March 23, 2010; AFP, Yemen Women Oppose Proposed Child Marriage Ban, *Khaleej Times Online*, March 21, 2010; "'Bone Ache' and Depression—The Lot of Child Brides," *Yemen Times*, September 2, 2010.

143. Clark, p. 171.

144. It is probably not surprising under these circumstances that Yemen ranks last in the world on the World Economic Forums "gender gap rankings" which measures women's equality on various levels including economic opportunities, educational attainment, health and survival issues, and political empowerment. See Richardo Hausmann, Laura D. Tyson, and Saadia Zahidi, *The Global Gender Gap Report 2010*, Geneva, Switzerland: World Economic Forum 2010, available from *www.weforum.org*.

145. Johnsen "The Expansion Strategy of Al-Qa'ida in the Arabian Peninsula," p. 8.

146. Sean O'Neill, "Land of 60 million guns gave bin Laden the cold shoulder," *Telegraph*, London, October 8, 2010.

147. Clark, pp. 159, 282.

148. *Ibid.*, p. 159.

149. Jonathan Randal, *Osama, The Making of a Terrorist*, New York: Alfred A. Knopf, 2004, p. 100.

150. Clark, p. 161.

151. Watkins, p. 8.

152. Dresch, p. 142.

153. Lacey, pp. 148-149.

154. Thomas R. Mockaitis, *Osama Bin Laden: A Biography*, Santa Barbara, CA: Greenwood Press, 2010, p. 52.

155. Steve Coll, *The Bin Ladens: An Arabian Family in the American Century*, New York: Penguin, 2008, pp. 301-303.

156. Robert Lacey, *Inside the Kingdom*, New York: Viking, 2009, pp. 148-149.

157. Bruce Riedel, *The Search for Al-Qaeda: Its Leadership, Ideology, and Future*, Washington, DC, 2008, p. 47.

158. Peter L. Bergen, *Holy War Inc.*, New York: The Free Press, 2001, p. 172.

159. Day, "Updating Yemeni National Unity," p. 421.

160. On the Jordanian example, see Jean-Charles Brisard, with Damien Martinez, *Zarqawi, The New Face of Al-Qaeda*, New York: Other Press, 2005, p. 41.

161. Brynjar Lia, *Architect of Global Jihad: The Life of Al-Qaida Strategist Abu Mus'ab al-Suri*, New York: Columbia University Press, 2008, p. 107.

162. *MECS*, Vol. XXI, 1997, p. 769.

163. Lacey, *Inside the Kingdom*, pp. 204-206.

164. Clark, p. 163.

165. *Ibid.*, pp. 166-167.

166. Jeremy M. Sharp, *Yemen: Background and U.S. Relations*, Washington, DC: Congressional Research Service, January 13, 2010, pp. 8, 25.

167. *Ibid.*, p. 173.

168. Clark, p. 167.

169. Gregory D. Johnsen, "The Resiliency of Yemen's Aden-Abyan Islamic Army," *Jamestown Foundation Terrorism Monitor*, July 13, 2006; Michael Knights, "Internal politics complicate counterterrorism in Yemen," *Jane's Intelligence Review*, February 1, 2006.

170. *The 9/11 Commission Report*, New York: W. W. Norton & Company, 2004, pp. 190-191.

171. Clark, pp. 166-167.

172. *The 9/11 Commission Report*, pp. 231-232.

173. Clark, p. 282.

174. *Ibid.*, p. 223.

175. Gregory D. Johnsen, "AQAP in Yemen and the Christmas Day Terrorist Attack," *West Point Counter Terrorism Center Sentinel*, January 2010, p. 5. This strike may have remained a CIA secret had it not been for the actions of U.S. Deputy Secretary of Defense Paul Wolfowitz, who on behalf of the Bush administration seemed to take credit for the strike in a CNN interview shortly before the U.S. mid-term elections. See "Wolfowitz: U.S. missile strike kills al-Qaeda chief," *CNN.com*, November 5, 2002.

176. *Ibid.*

177. Gregory D. Johnsen, "Al-Qaeda makes a new mark in Yemen," *Asia Times Online*, July 4, 2007.

178. Clark, p. 227.

179. *Ibid.*

180. Johnsen, "AQAP in Yemen and the Christmas Day Terrorist Attack," p. 5.

181. Gordon Lubold, "New Look at Foreign Fighters in Iraq," *Christian Science Monitor*, January 7, 2008.

182. Joseph Felter and Brian Fishman, *Al-Qaida's Foreign Fighters in Iraq: A First Look at the Sinjar Records*, West Point, NY: Center

for Combating Terrorism, 2008, pp. 7-8. See Ed Blanche, "An Al-Qaeda Rolodex," *The Middle East*, March 2008, pp. 7-10.

183. See Blanche, "An Al-Qaeda rolodex," pp. 7-10; Clark, p. 203.

184. "Yemen Frees 170 al-Qaeda Suspects," *Saudi Gazette*, February 9, 2009.

185. "US orders embassy staff to leave Yemen," *Kuwait Times*, April 9, 2008.

186. Ahmed al-Haj, "Yemen upholds death sentences in U.S. Embassy attack," *Washington Times*, July 11, 2010.

187. "Yemen Qaeda claims attack on UK Envoy," *Gulf Times*, May 13, 2010.

188. Michael Isikoff, "Deadly Training Ground," *Newsweek*, September 17, 2008, available from *www.newsweek.com*.

189. Yemeni authorities maintain that three of the attackers had recently returned from Iraq. See "US Embassy Attacked Said Linked to Al-Qaeda," *Washington Post*, November 2, 2008.

190. Isikoff.

191. Michael Scheuer, "Yemen still close to al-Qaeda's heart," *Asia Times Online*, February 7, 2008.

192. Christopher Boucek, *Yemen: Avoiding a Downward Spiral*, Carnegie Paper No. 102, Washington, DC: Carnegie Endowment of International Peace, 2009, p. 12.

193. *Ibid.*, p. 12.

194. "Yemen arrests 29 al-Qaeda suspects after raids," *Reuters*, December 29, 2009.

195. Eric Schmitt and Scott Shane, "Christmas Bombing Try is Hailed by bin Laden," *New York Times*, January 25, 2010.

196. Sarah Wheaton, "Obama Plays Down Military Role in Yemen," *New York Times*, January 11, 2010.

197. *Ibid.*

198. "Yemen warned against 'occupation,'" BBC News Online, January 11, 2010.

199. "Obama Approves Secret Operations in Yemen," *Kuwait Times*, January 28, 2010; "The Secret War in Yemen," *Yemen Times*, September 2, 2010.

200. Robert Worth, "Is Yemen the Next Afghanistan?" *New York Times Magazine*, July 6, 2010, available from *www.nytimes.com*.

201. *Ibid.*

202. "Barack Obama praises Yemen's fight against al-Qa'eda," Telegraph Media Group, July 16, 2010.

203. Nadia al-Sakkkaf, "Al-Qaeda Steps Up its Tactics as the Government Strikes Harder," *Yemen Times*, September 16, 2010.

204. *Ibid.*

205. *Ibid.*

206. Mohammad Bin Sallam, "21 Killed in Confrontations in Abyan, *Yemen Times*, August 23, 2010.

207. Worth, *New York Times Magazine*.

208. Joanna Sugden, "Hundreds of al-Qaeda militants planning attacks from Yemen," Times Online, *London Sunday Times*, December 29, 2009, available from *www.timesonline.co.uk*.

209. Henry Meyer, "Al-Qaeda Claims Failed Attack on U.K Envoy to Yemen, SITE Says," May 12, 2010, available from *Bloomberg.com*.

210. On Pakistanis in Yemen, see "Yemen says town free of Qaeda grip," *Gulf Times*, August 25, 2010.

211. Charles Levinson and Margaret Coker, "Al-Qaeda's Deep Tribal Ties Make Yemen a Terror Hub," *Wall Street Journal*, January 22, 2010, p. 1.

212. "Yemen says town free of Qaeda Grip."

213. *Ibid.;* "Obama's other surge — in Yemen," *Christian Science Monitor*, August 25, 2010.

214. "Yemen says seven Qaeda members among 21 killed in south," AFP, August 21, 2010.

215. "Yemen army 'regains control' of southern town," AFP, August 25, 2010.

216. Casualties were reported as in the "dozens," which is not high for urban combat involving significant numbers of troops. It is, however, possible that the government has minimized security forces casualties. See Agence France Presse, "Thousands Protest 'blockage' of south Yemen city Loder," *Daily Star*, September 17, 2010.

217. Robert F. Worth, "Yemen Military Attacks Town it Says is Militant Hide-out," *New York Times*, September 21, 2010.

218. "Thousands flee fighting in Yemen's Shabwa province," BBC News Online, September 20, 2010.

219. "Al-Qaeda militants using human shields in Yemen town — official," *Jordan Times*, September 22, 2010.

220. "Death toll rise to 12 in Yemen army post attack," Agence France Presse, AFP, August 30, 2010; "Eight troops die in south Yemen al-Qaeda attack," *Gulf Times*, August 29, 2010.

221. "Eight troops die in south Yemen al-Qaeda attack."

222. "Three police killed in Yemen attack, " United Press International, August 26, 2010.

223. "Gunmen attack two southern Yemen security offices," BBC News, July 14, 2010.

224. Nadia al-Sakkaf, "Al-Qaeda steps up its tactics as the government strikes harder," *Yemen Times*, September 16, 2010; Robert F. Worth, "Yemen Military Besieges Remote Qaeda Redoubt," *New York Times*, September 21, 2010.

225. See, for example, "Yemeni police chief shot dead," *Gulf Today*, October 15, 2010.

226. Agence France Presse, AFP, "Yemen tribesmen to stop harboring Qaeda suspects, " *Daily Star*, June 14, 2010.

227. Riedel, pp. 122-124.

228. Clark, p. 96.

229. Patrick E. Tyler, "Yemen, an Uneasy Ally, Proves Adept at Playing Off Old Rivals," *New York Times*, December 19, 2002.

230. Bob Woodward, *Bush at War*, New York: Simon & Schuster, 2003, p. 327.

231. Boucek, *Yemen Avoiding a Downward Spiral*, p. 14; Jeremy M. Sharp, *Yemen: Background and U.S. Relations*, Washington, DC: Congressional Research Service, January 13, 2010, p. 9.

232. Sharp.

233. *Ibid.* Article 44 of the Yemeni Constitution states that a citizen of Yemen may not be extradited to a foreign country for prosecution under foreign laws.

234. Several Yemenis have told the author that in Yemen kinship and tribe are much more important than religion. While such attitudes are not uncommon throughout the Islamic world, it is unusual for anyone to admit this reality, especially when not prompted to do so.

235. Ester Schrader and Henry Weinstein, "U.S. Enters a Legal Gray Zone, *Los Angeles Times*, November 5, 2002.

236. Gregory D. Johnsen, "Al-Qa'ida in Yemen's 2008 Campaign, *Counter Terrorism Center Sentinel*, January 2010, p. 13.

237. *Ibid.*

238. "Two Killed as thousands protest around the World," *Sidney Morning Herald*, March 22, 2003. In March 2003 demonstrators reported to be in the "tens of thousands" marched on the U.S. embassy and were stopped by Yemeni security forces, with at least two dead.

239. Mohamed Sudam, "Yemen rejects bigger US role in al-Qaeda fight," *Daily Star*, August 27, 2010; Kimberly Dozier, "Officials: CIA drones may target Yemen terrorists," Associated Press, August 25, 2010.

240. Gregory D. Johnsen, "The Expansion Strategy of al-Qa'ida in the Arabian Peninsula," *Counter Terrorism Center Sentinel*, September 2009, p. 8.

241. Sarah A. Topol, "Why Yemen's US-aided fight against al-Qaeda could backfire," *Christian Science Monitor*, April 30, 2010.

242. Tony Capaccio, "Military Aid to Yemen Doubles as U.S. Aims to Boost Fight against al-Qaeda," *Blooomberg.com*, August 25, 2010.

243. *Ibid.*

244. "Obama Promises Justice for Christmas Terror Plotters," *CNN.com*, January 2, 2010.

245. Sugden.

246. "Yemen warned against 'occupation'," *BBC News*, January 11, 2010.

247. Office of Public Affairs, U.S. Department of the Treasury, "United States Designates bin Laden Loyalist," Press Release JS-1190, February 24, 2004.

248. Robert F. Worth, "Cleric in Yemen Admits Meeting Airline Plot Suspect, Journalist Says," *New York Times*, February 1, 2010.

249. Office of the Press Secretary, The White House, "Readout of the President's Call with President Saleh of Yemen," Press Release, July 15, 2010.

250. Agence France-Presse, "Obama applauds Yemen's anti-terror watch," Gulf Research Center; Gulf in the Media, July 16, 2010.

251. "Obama stresses support for 'unified' Yemen," *The Peninsula*, Qatar, September 21, 2010.

252. "Yemen militants kill 11 in brazen jailbreak," *Kuwait Times*, June 20, 2010.

253. Marisa L. Porges, "De-radicalization, the Yemeni Way," *Survival*, Vol. 52, No. 2, April-May 2010, p. 28.

254. For a more detailed exploration of these issues, see W. Andrew Terrill, *Global Security Watch Jordan*, Santa Barbara, CA: Praeger, 2010, pp. 42-44.

www.ingramcontent.com/pod-product-compliance
Lightning Source LLC
Chambersburg PA
CBHW070202290526
45789CB00002B/873